NOTE: Page 4, after 2nd para:an application has been made to divert the path so that it follows the stream.

Steps to the A4, Batheaston

KEY TO SYMBOLS

	the path
	not this way
	field boundaries
	dismantled railway track
	working railway
	trees
S	stile
G	gate
K/G	kissing gate
Bg	bridge
F/P	footpath
B/way	bridleway
P H	public house
P O	post office
+	church
T.R.,T.L.	turn right, turn left
R.H.,L.H.	right hand, left hand
X	route continues at next X

NORTH is always at the top of the page

The scale of the maps is approximately
4" to 1 mile

The area is covered by Ordnance Survey Pathfinder maps $2\frac{1}{2}$" to 1 mile (1:25,000) as follows:

ST 67/77 Bristol (East)
ST 66/76 Bath and Keynsham
ST 65/75 Radstock and Wellow
ST 45/55 Cheddar

INTRODUCTION

The 'Limestone Link' is a route of 36 miles joining the limestone of the Cotswolds to that of the Mendip Hills. It is a connecting route between the Cotswold Way at Cold Ashton and the West Mendip Way at Shipham. Between the two, the route passes through the valleys and villages south of Bath. Except for an ascent at each end, the walk is mostly flat and not strenuous.

Included are 12 circular walks varying in length from three to twelve miles, each using a part of the 'Link'.

Cyril Trenfield, of the Avon Area Ramblers'Association, was inspired to devise the 'Link' by a reference in a Wansdyke District Council Structure Plan to the desirability of having such a path running across the south part of Avon & connecting with the Cotswold Way. It was walked, written and published by Yatton Ramblers who have endeavoured to provide correct and accurate routes; no responsibility can be accepted for any errors or omissions. Distances are approximate and are given as a guide.

If a walker encounters a problem he should report it to Cyril Trenfield at 38 Oakdale Court, Downend, Bristol BS16 6DU. Copies of the book may be obtained from this address-please add 35p. postage.

Yatton Ramblers wish to thank the staff of the County of Avon Public Rights of Way Department for their ever-willing help on footpath matters.

May we please ask walkers to observe the Country Code, in particular closing gates, causing no damage, keeping dogs under control and leaving no litter.

1. Cold Ashton to Batheaston

The path follows the course of St.Catherine's Brook to the R. Avon.
Distance: 5 miles

The Cotswold Way comes into Cold Ashton on the path by the side of the church. T.R. on reaching road, and in a few yards, opp.gate of Old Rectory, L. through iron gate into field. Down this steep field towards trees at bottom. Over stile into small enclosure with springs. Right on down to bottom of valley, cross stream, T.L. and keep on track beside stream (on left).

At bottom, through gate in R.H. hedge and R. on rough narrow path with another stream on L. Into field and double back again above this stream(still on your L). Through gate and on over field,through next gate, on with hedge on your L., path soon becomes track. Keep on this track (ignore arrow on post by concrete/iron tank) under electric wires, through iron gate and keep on lane to road.

T.L. and L. again at once at F/P post. Through gate and down ridge in field, straight on. At bottom by stream over stile in corner. Cross lane to stile opp.by building (Beek's Mill). Keep parallel to and above stream on your R., crossing in turn a stile, double stile with bridge, and stile. Then over a large field to iron gate by stream. NOT up track to L. but along by stream via stile by broken iron gate and next gate to road at F/P sign.

L. on road up hill and R. at F/P sign before house (Ayford). This is a muddy and overgrown track which led to the former mill. Keep between hedges by a stream to stile. Cross track, over wooden fence ahead, through small wood, over stream and

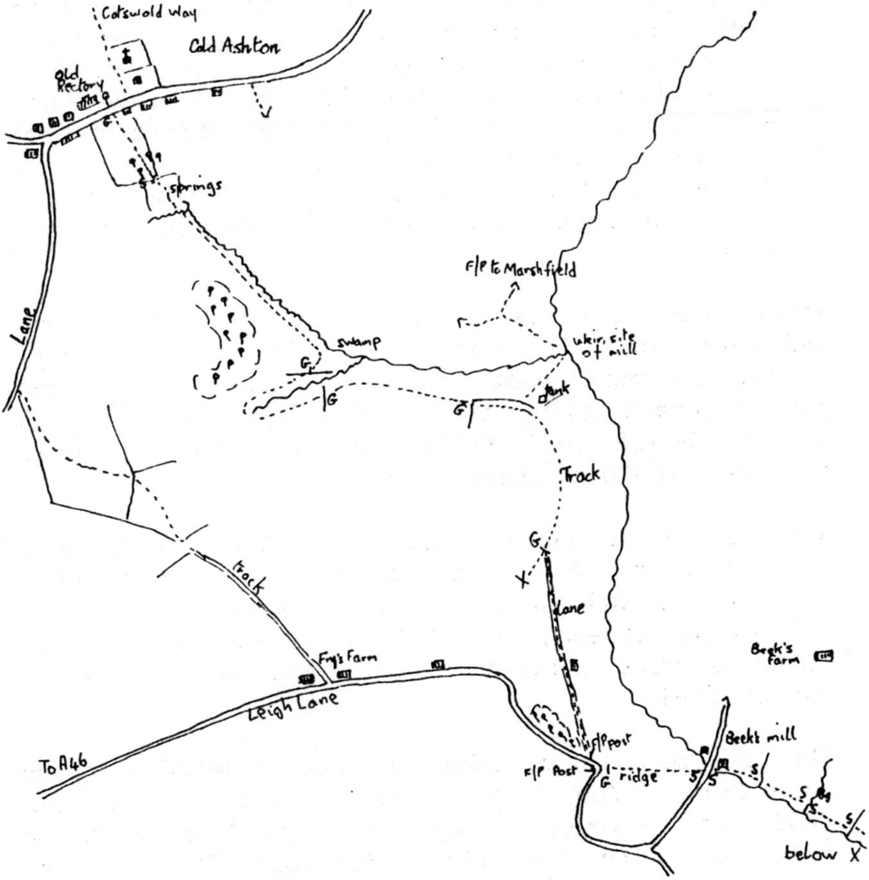
Cotswold Way
Cold Ashton
Old Rectory
springs
Lane
F/P to Marshfield
swamp
weir, site of mill
Track
Track
Lane
Beek's Farm
Fry's Farm
Leigh Lane
To A46
F/P Post
F/P Post
ridge
Beek's mill
below X

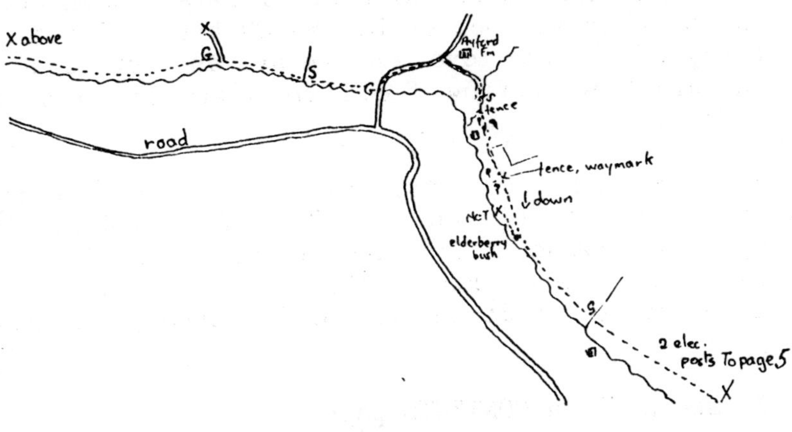
X above
road
Ayford Fm
fence
fence, waymark
down
elderberry bush
2 elec. posts
To page 5

up muddy path. Over wooden pole fence into field (waymark) and on a few yards until St.Catherine's Court comes into view on your R. Then bear R.downhill to stream. For those walking in the other direction, do not go along by the stream beyond the large elderberry bush because the way ahead is overgrown, but climb up round the edge of the field to the trees, and over the wooden pole fence, as above.

After next stile go slightly L. away from stream and make for elec. post in middle of field (waymark), to next post opp.Court, bear up L. and join a track going to L. of ash trees. Through gap in hedge (old stile) and on the rise make for the buildings ahead. X

When track is reached near old barn, T.R. down it and soon (bottom of slope) over wire fence on your R. and to the L. of 2 stiles - i.e. do NOT cross stream, but follow it on narrow path round a hill (stream on R.) and over stile at end of field.

The $2\frac{1}{2}$" map is mistaken in not showing a green path here. You keep by the stream to the next road, as follows: cross track leading to house (old pub with lettering 'Benjamin Blaman') and ahead through small white metal gate. Down driveway by chicken coop on L. WATCH here. T.L.before bridge. Stiles over driveway and straight on through long narrow field to stile by iron gate to road. *

For the Mead Tea Gardens go up R. to road junction and T.R. and it's on your R. a few hundred yards up. Otherwise, T.R. and immed.L. at F/P post past iron gate into field. Stream now on your L. - stile by it in far L.H. corner, to track.

X see NOTE on CONTENTS page.

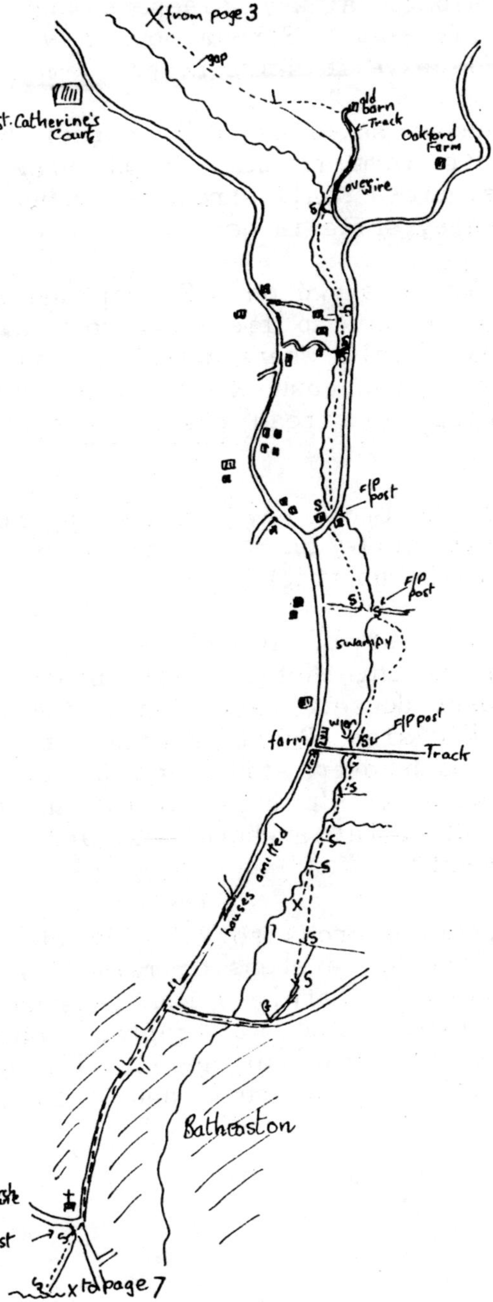
X from page 3
gap
St. Catherine's Court
old barn
Track
Oakford Farm
over wire
S
F/P post
S
F/P post
swampy
wlgn
S
F/P post
farm
Track
S
S
S
houses omitted
X
S
S
Batheaston
Church Lane
F/P post
X to page 7

L. here along railway sleepers and over stile on R. by F/P post. Stream now on your R. again, but you will have to skirt round swampy area.

In next hedge stile in R.H. corner by F/P post and weir to farm track. On through iron gate, then stile, cross small stream on stepping stones, stile by gate, stile in hedge.

Now leave route shown on O.S. map and go to stile in hedge half way up field on your L. Cross to top of next field where stile is on L.H. side, then follow path down R. to iron gate to road (if you keep to stream there is no way out to road).

If walking the other way, on leaving road at iron gate, ignore stile on R. just through this gate and go straight up track.

T.R. up road and L. at top down main street to Batheaston church. Notice Eagle House, Pine House and Middlesex House. Past church and over Church Lane, see F/P sign 'Public Footpath to Bailbrook'. Take this path over stile and by L.H. hedge to stile by stream. Up hill to L. and to road by the former Hill Farm, where T.L. and down (notice stone pavement).

At road junction cross to R.C. church, down steep path to L. ending in steps to main A4 road. Buses run from here to Bath. T.L., passing shops and two pubs, cross road at traffic lights to F/P sign by toilets and car park. Through squeeze stile at end of car park and onto path which runs beside R. Avon.

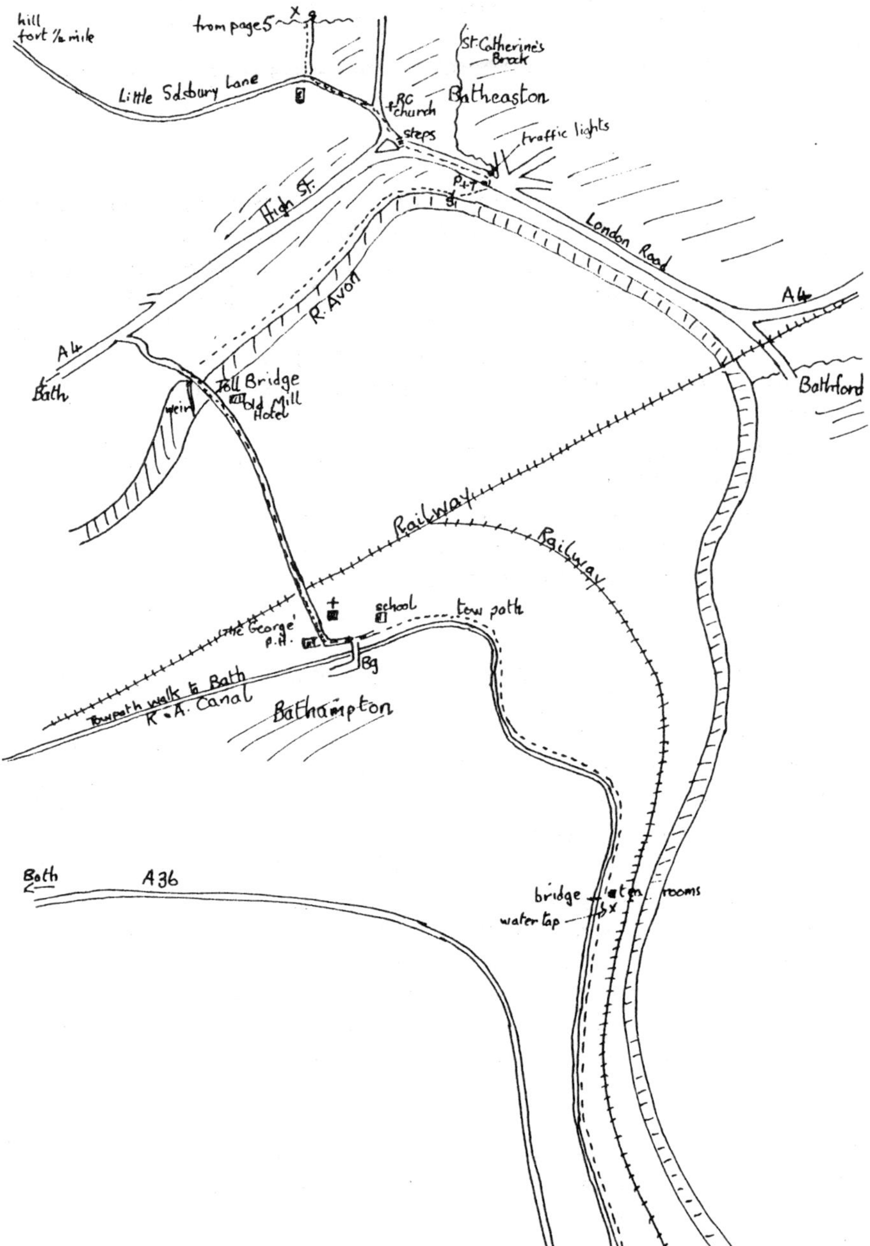

hill fort ½ mile
from page 5
Little Solsbury Lane
RC church
St. Catherine's Brook
Batheaston
steps
traffic lights
P+T
High St.
London Road
R. Avon
A4
A4
Bath
Toll Bridge
Old Mill Hotel
weir
Bathford
Railway
Railway
'The George' P.H.
school
tow path
Bg
Towpath walk to Bath
K. A. Canal
Bathampton
Bath
A36
bridge
tea rooms
water tap
to page 9

2. Batheaston to Midford

This includes a pleasant walk along the Kennet and Avon Canal towpath.
Distance: 6 miles

Walk along by the river and on reaching road T.L. over toll bridge. Notice old tariff board. Along the road to Bathampton, as far as the church on L. and 'The George' on R. Road bends L. here and just before it crosses the canal bridge leave it, and opp. the primary school join towpath of Kennet & Avon Canal. Keep on this for 3 miles, passing:

1. Bridge by teashop and water tap in $\frac{3}{4}$ mile;
2. Second bridge;
3. Claverton pumping station, see notice on L.
4. Third bridge - access to Claverton village and American Museum.
5. Fourth bridge.

On reaching Dundas Aqueduct basin, cross over canal by footbridge. Go behind building to crane - aqueduct is to L. and bridge in front is the start of the Somerset Coal Canal. See information board as you go up track on your R. to A36 road. T.L. on road, pass garage, to traffic lights.

At traffic lights (opp. pub) T.L. down B3108. At bottom of slope before you reach the bridge, over stile by iron gate on R.H. side (F/P post). The path doubles back under the A36. Keep to R.H. side of Monkton Combe School playing fields; near the end of these take short track up R. to tarred road.

L. and immed. R. up path through wood by stone wall (before reaching gate marked 'Monkton Combe School, Longmead'). At end of path cross road and up steps opp., ahead via K/G.

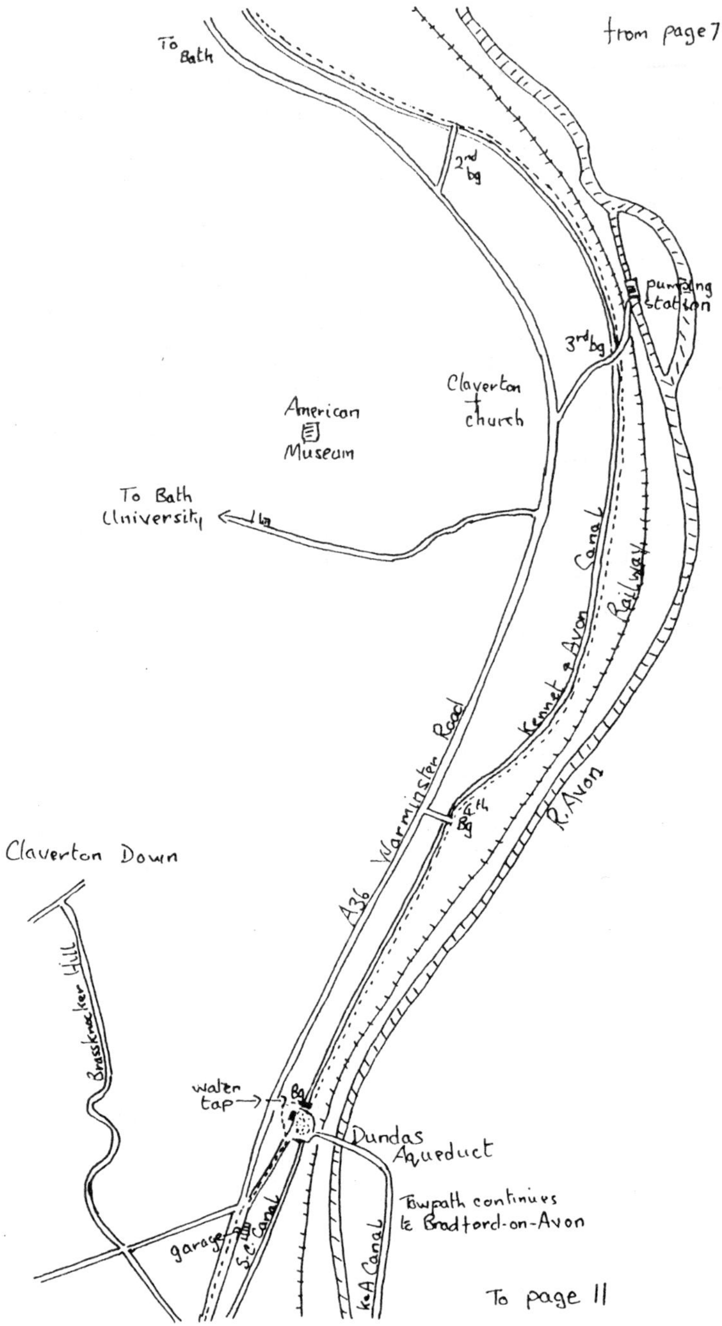

from page 7
To Bath
2nd bg
pumping station
3rd bg
Claverton church
American Museum
To Bath University
Kennet & Avon Canal
Railway
A36 Warminster Road
4th Bg
R. Avon
Claverton Down
Brassknocker Hill
water tap
Bg
Dundas Aqueduct
Towpath continues to Bradford-on-Avon
garage
S.C. Canal
K&A Canal
To page 11

Up slope. Keep school buildings on your L. On to iron K/G right at top, to road at F/P sign. T.L. and go through village. Road bears R. and L. round church. At next turning, L. on road to Tucking Mill and Midford. (You can walk through the churchyard instead and come out on this road. If you do, then T.L.).

On road for ½ mile; on reaching buildings - Tucking Mill - * see low stone F/P marker on L. and go through wooden gate here. High hedge on R. Over stile. See cottage on R. over road, which once stood on canal bank, and has notice 'William Smith, Father of English Geology'. Path goes between fence on L. and road on R.

Over stile and keep on path through wood for about ¼ mile. Out onto road (B3110) by iron gate and F/P sign. This is Midford. T.R. on road and cross it opp. 'Hope & Anchor'.

Here take path which goes under the old Somerset and Dorset Railway bridge, with a garden on your L. Over stile. The path follows the old canal bank. The stone bridge on your L. led to the canal basin. Over stile and bend round L. to two more stiles.

Here L. in a wet and muddy area and under another railway arch.

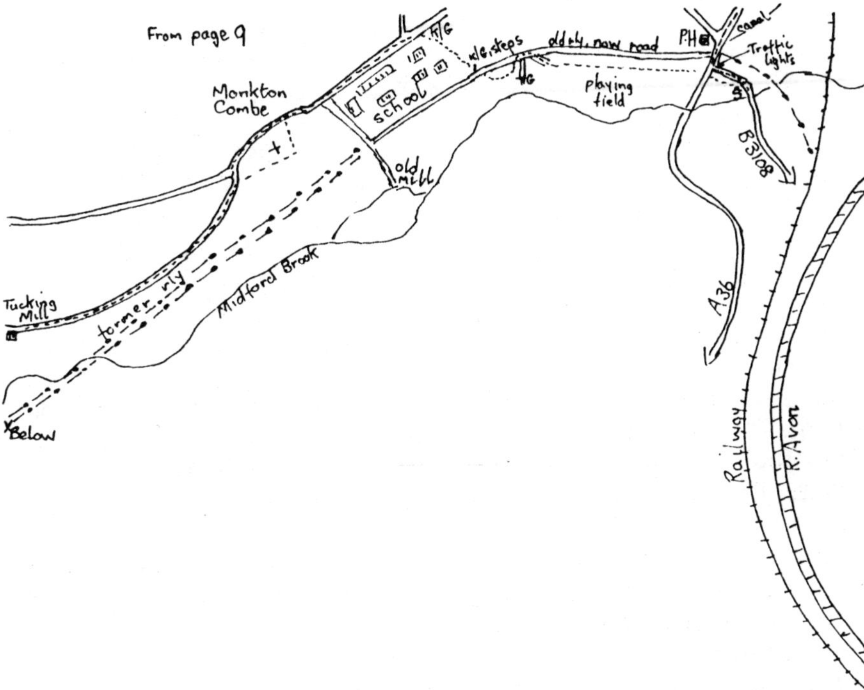
From page 9
Monkton Combe
K/G
school
old Mill
old rly, now road
steps
G
P.H
canal
Traffic lights
playing field
S
B3108
A36
Railway
R. Avon
Tucking Mill
former rly
Midford Brook
Below

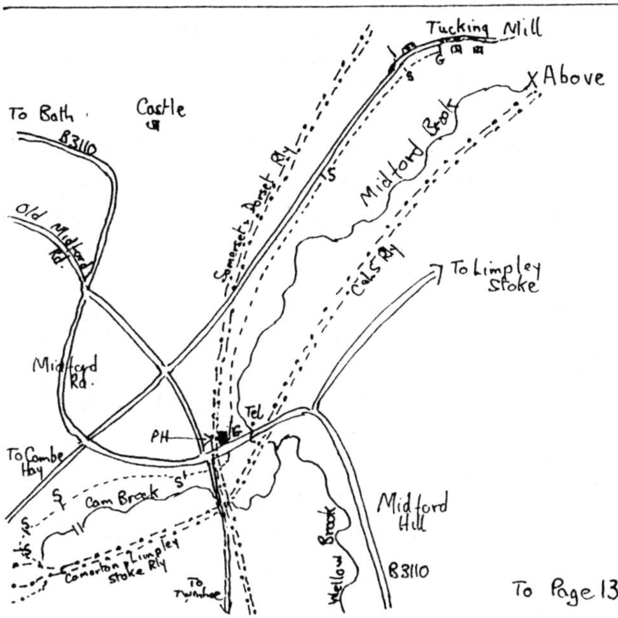
Tucking Mill
Above
G
S
To Bath
Castle
B3110
Old Midford Rd.
Somerset & Dorset Rly
Midford Brook
C&LS Rly
To Limpley Stoke
Midford Rd.
PH
Tel
To Combe Hay
Cam Brook
Camerton Limpley Stoke Rly
To Twinhoe
Wellow Brook
Midford Hill
B3110
To Page 13

3. Midford to Dunkerton

The path follows the course of the Cam Brook and of the old canal and railway.
Distance: 4½ miles

Having gone under the railway, T.R. and NOT into field by stream, but over stile on L. a few yards further on, into field. Follow round contour of old canal bed for approx. ½ mile.

At end, stile in R.H. corner of field onto track, where R. and immed. L. over stile (canal wall here under vegetation). Next stile into narrow field - siteof 2 more locks - past sheds on R., through metal gate before reaching house. Then bear R. to stile onto road (F/P post).

Cross road and go under arch of old railway and on to stile by gate. Path goes straight on with fence on R. and flight of locks of old canal on L. Over next stile into wooded area, ignoring F/B on your L., soon opening out into a field. Here, see tree on L. with waymark and go L. over stream. If you can see the ruined house across the field you have gone too far.

Double back over muddy area to stile in wire fence. Bear L. and climb steeply to double stile at top. Up next field bearing R. to double stile under tree (L. of piece of fencing) in far hedge. Sharp L. here. If you are coming the other way, T.L. when over stile,ignoring path ahead also waymarked. Caisson House is down on your L. and view of South Stoke church in distance behind. Path turns into track, passing Rowley Farm, and on to road. Here T.R. into Combe Hay, passing pub on your R.

Walk through the village, and past the old school house T.L. at stile in stone wall (F/P post).

From page 11

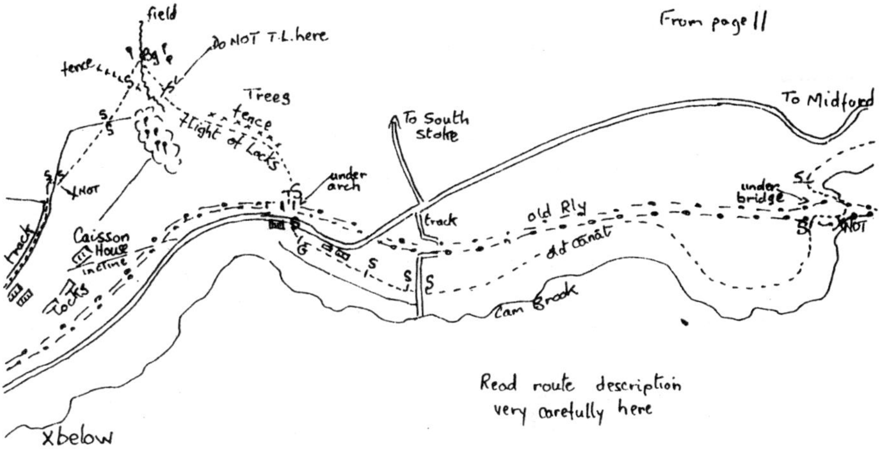

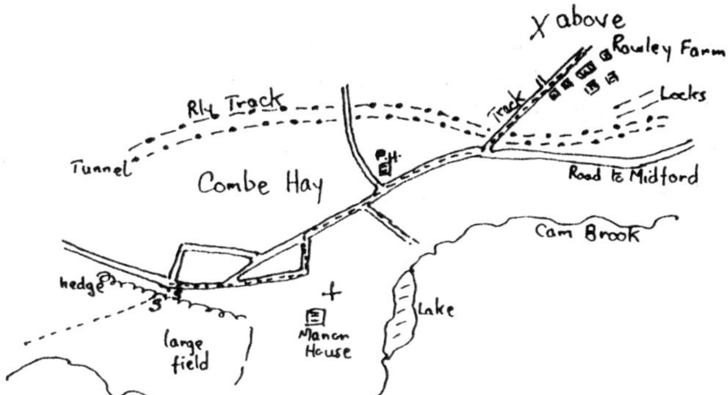

To page 15

Another stile into field. Bear $\frac{1}{2}$ R. ahead to far corner of large field down by stream; stile by gate to road.

T.R. on road and immed. L. through metal gate into field. Path goes slightly L. to bank of Cam Brook. Then keep by stream for about 1 mile, when the main road (A367) comes into view in front of you. Do NOT bear round R. to gate, but straight on and up flight of stone steps to this road, at Dunkerton Bridge.

Cross this busy road with care and down another flight of stone steps. Keeping the stream on your R. make for Dunkerton church. Go through gate into field just before church, cross field with church on your L. and out at K/G onto lane by bridge. Cross lane and over stone stile.

Now keep on for about 1 mile with stream always on your R., as follows: cross two stiles in succession, then a third one by an iron gate. Through the next iron gate, then a double stile. Now another iron gate.

Near the end of the next field take the iron gate on your R. and over a bridge onto the road, where T.L. This is easier than going to the end of the field and on a short path to the road, as the path may be overgrown.

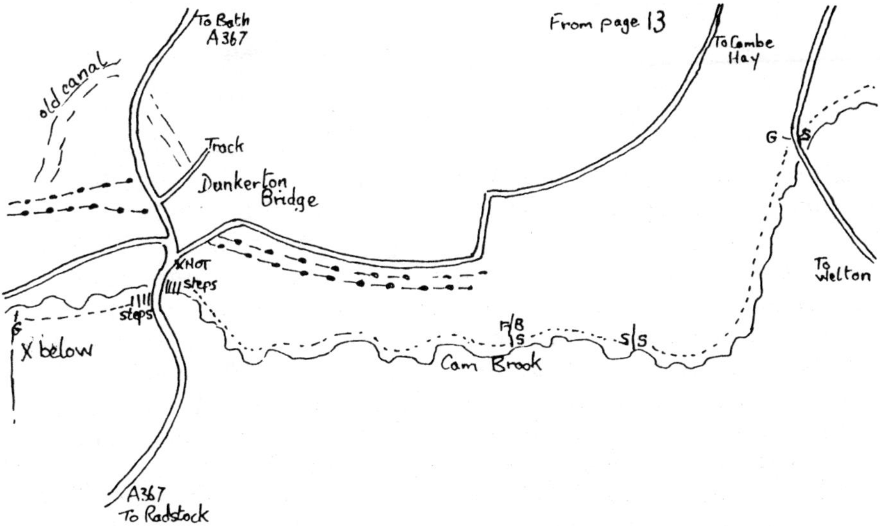
To Bath
A367
From page 13
To Combe Hay
old canal
Track
Dunkerton Bridge
G
S
To Welton
X NOT steps
steps
steps
X below
F/B
S
S|S
Cam Brook
A367
To Radstock

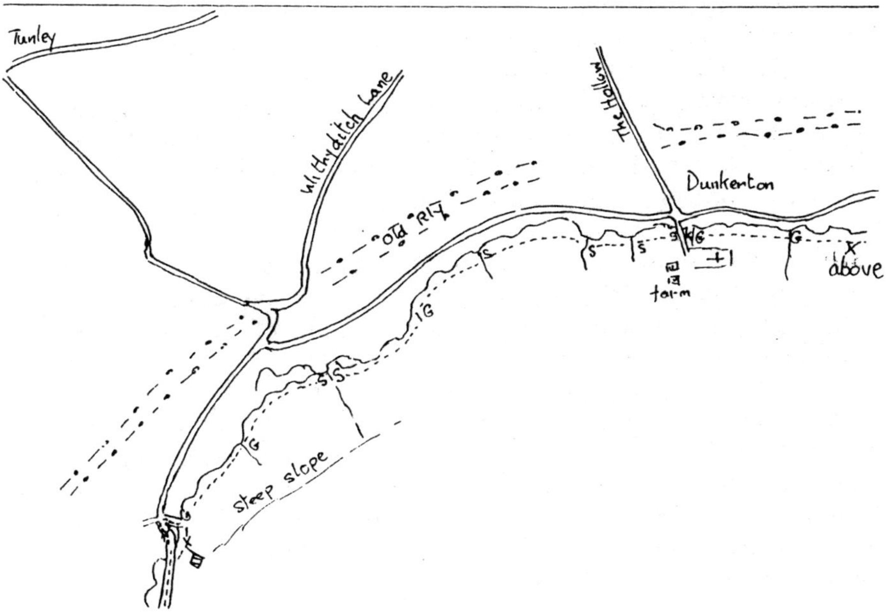
Tunley
Withyditch Lane
The Hollow
Dunkerton
Old Rly
S
S
S
G
G
X above
farm
G
S|S
G
steep slope
To page 17

4. Dunkerton to Clutton

Past old colliery sites and through the canal basin at Paulton.
Distance: $6\frac{1}{4}$ miles

Along road for a few hundred yards and R. on B/way before large pylon, stream on your R. Cross it, through wooden gate, then gate to road. T.R. and almost immed. L. through K/G, opp. house gate. Up track over field and soon see stile up bank on R. Cross, and follow path to L. on old railway track for about $\frac{1}{4}$ mile. At end, NOT down L., but R. on dark path under bushes to K/G by house. Down in front of house and bear R. where lane bends L. Then L. round back of other houses. Keep slightly up slope in field but after last house, down to wire fence and stile.

T.R., keep wire fence on your R., towards old colliery tip. Walk round it (it is on your L.), but half way round leave track, over stile on L. (NOT the one ahead). Keep fence on L. and through iron gate into old mine yard. Straight on in front of a house on your R., to tarmac track ahead. At end emerge onto road between houses and old chapel, opp. Camerton post office.

Cross road and take track by telephone box, not through the gate but to L. of it between fence and back gardens (old towpath) until wooden K/G and gate into garden are reached.

Walk right through the middle of the garden, via another wicket gate and straight on, keeping up high on towpath to another wooden K/G and tarmac track. Double back - i.e., sharply L., in front of house, under former railway bridge and out on the road.

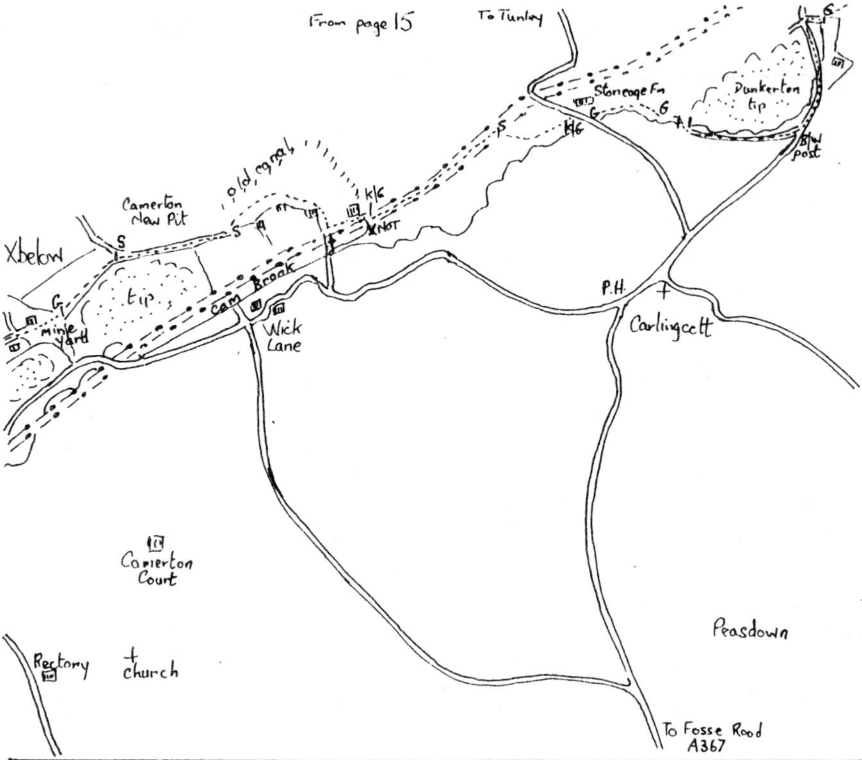
From page 15
To Tunley
Stoneage Fm
Dunkerton tip
old canal
Camerton New Pit
X below
tip
Cam Brook
mine yard
Wick Lane
P.H.
Carlingcott
Camerton Court
Peasdown
Rectory
church
To Fosse Road A367

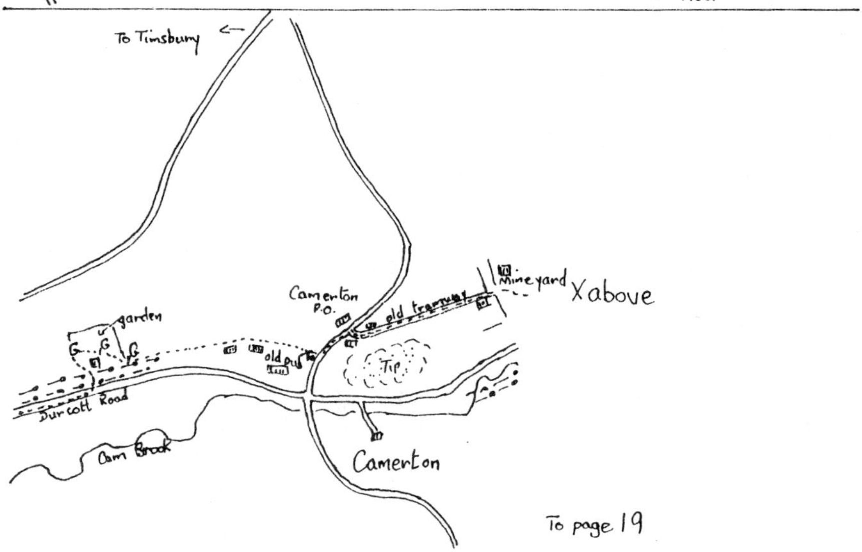
To Timsbury
mine yard
X above
Camerton P.O.
old tramway
garden
old pub
Tip
Durcott Road
Cam Brook
Camerton
To page 19

T.R. and walk on road to T-junction at Radford where L., then R.H. fork (marked Paulton and Midsomer Norton). Soon T.R., cross stream and down track. Bear L. behind farm buildings. Over stile ahead and forward on path parallel with old railway line (on your R.).

Stile by iron gate and then bear R. to just L. of oak tree, ignoring stile on R. Cross a track and straight on in damp depression (canal bed) to next stile. On with fence on your L., pass colliery tip away on R. across hedge of old railway track to stile with dog flap.

Here you are in the Paulton canal basin area and there is a large number of paths, owing to former industrial activity, and care is needed to find the way.

The obvious way is to go forward on the towing path with the canal bed on your R. to the next stile, then R. a few yards up a track and L. to bottom corner of hedge. However, the stile here is blocked and so use the iron gate at the top of the field against the old railway line, so it would be quicker to cross canal bed by stile with dog flap and go diag. R. across field to aforesaid iron gate in top R.H. corner. Ignore stile up here in top hedge.

Go back down (L.) and walk with old basin on your L. to two hawthorn bushes. Cross canal bed between them and ahead over stile and bridge (Cam Brook). Along path with tip on L. to sewage works.

Here T.R. down tarmac drive to road and over stile by metal gate. T.R. up the road to Goosard Bridge.

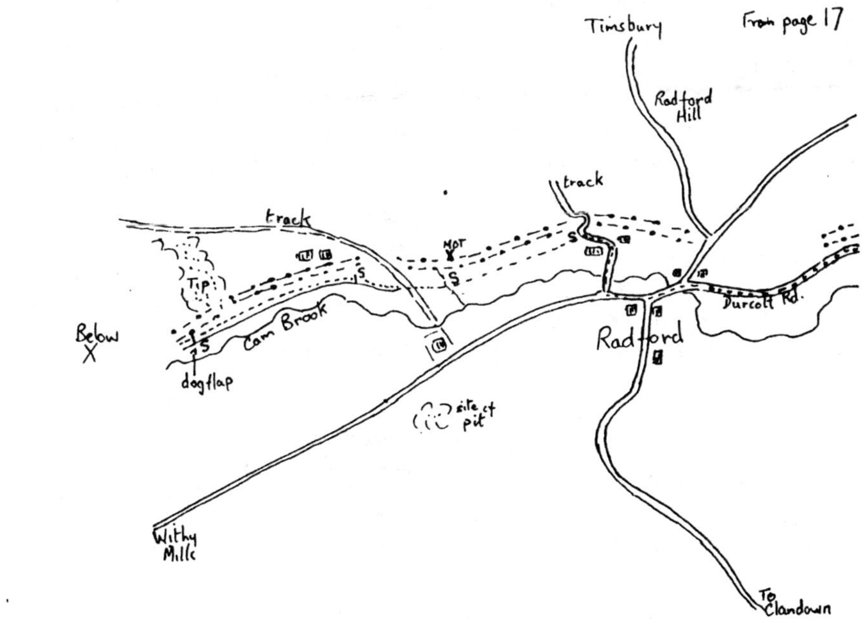
Timsbury
From page 17
Radford Hill
track
track
NOT
S
S
S
S
Tip
Below X
Cam Brook
dogflap
Radford
Durcott Rd.
site of pit
Withy Mills
To Clandown

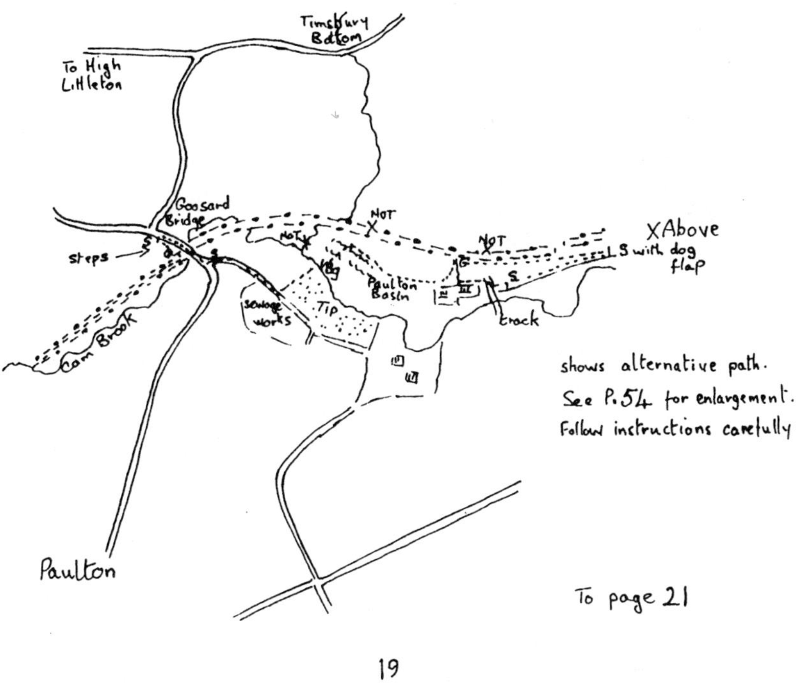
Timsbury Bottom
To High Littleton
Goosard Bridge
NOT
NOT
NOT
X Above
S with dog flap
steps
Paulton Basin
sewage works
Tip
S
track
Cam Brook
Paulton
shows alternative path.
See P.54 for enlargement.
Follow instructions carefully.
To page 21

Immed. over the bridge, T.L. down steps to stile and iron gate onto old railway track. See traces of old station platform. T.R. and walk on track for 1 mile. When track becomes blocked and houses are visible one field away on either side, go L. over wooden fence. T.R. to stile by gate and up to road at Hallatrow. For shop and pub, T.L.

To continue route, cross road to stone squeeze stile. Another stile at end of R.H. fence. Cross next field diag. R. Stile to old railway track, which path crosses diag. Over bridge.

Follow obvious path between two hills, stream on your L. Go on to F/B on your L., cross it, up slope and over stile. Do NOT go over next bridge, but keep on path to L. with stream on your R. and over stile.

The path skirts round bottom of the hill through bracken for ¼ mile, then over stile and leave stream. In next field, keep up at foot of slope and follow path to stile in middle of hedge - do not turn up L.

Straight on, over stile by metal gate. Make for gap in hedge ahead, then to stile by gate to old railway track. Cross this and straight on path towards Clutton church. Onto road at K/G and T.R., still going towards church.

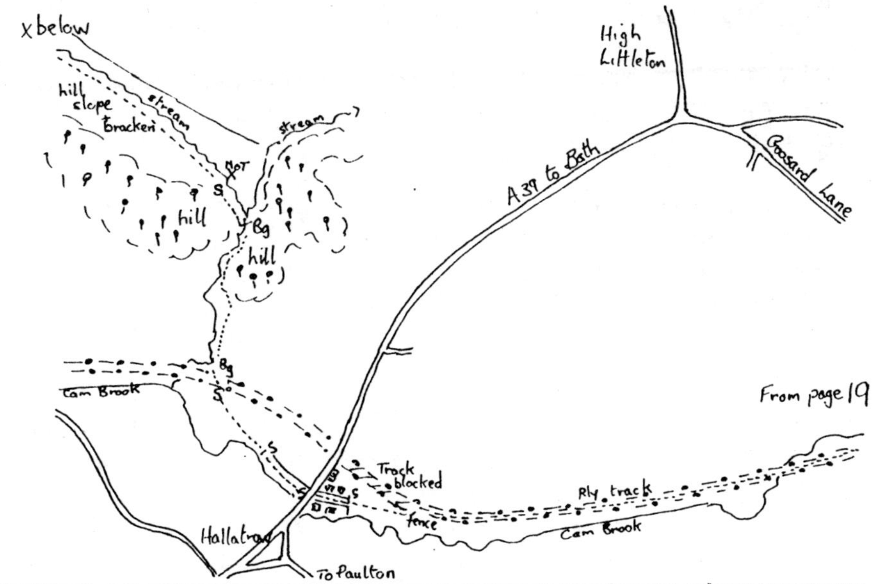
X below
hill
slope
bracken
stream
stream
NOT
S
hill
Bg
hill
High Littleton
A39 to Bath
Goosard Lane
Bg
Cam Brook
S
From page 19
S
Track blocked
S
Rly track
fence
Cam Brook
Hallatrow
To Paulton

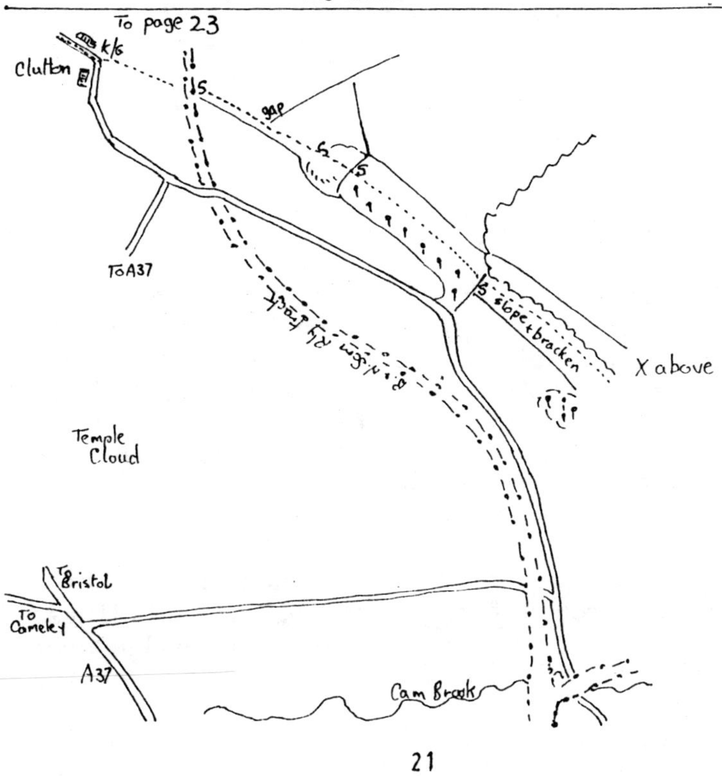
To page 23
K/G
Clutton
S
gap
S
S
To A37
S
slope + bracken
X above
Temple Cloud
To Bristol
To Cameley
A37
Cam Brook

5. Clutton to West Harptree

An area of steep fields and valleys where the path finally reaches the end of the Cam Brook.
Distance: $4\frac{3}{4}$ miles

Just before Clutton church T.L. via K/G and cross field aiming for space between trees. Half way over cross double stile and bridge, then on to iron K/G. Ignoring path straight on, fork R. and keep by stream all the way to the iron gate onto main A37 road.

T.R. and cross road to wooden field gate. Through garden, over double stile, ahead to gate. Straight up track with wood on your L. N.B. track not on O.S. map, and path has been officially diverted.

At top of slope track bends L.,but leave it and go R. up field, keeping to hedge on your R., to metal gate and stile. Diag. L. over next field to another gate and stile by oak tree at top of wood. Walk round top of wood keeping to edge of field to stile at end. (See Cameley church on L., here a path goes down the hill to it along edge of wood).

The route goes diag. R. to top of large field. Gate is hidden behind hedge. Through it and on for short way, then L. with top hedge on your R., following path to gate at lane. Do NOT go through it, but to stile in fence on your L. part way down slope (fence not on O.S. map). Then over field diag. to bottom corner, where T.L. on lane (Nanny Hurn's Lane).

At road, T.L. to corner (Cameley church is $\frac{1}{4}$ mile on) where R. through first gate, before buildings. Diag. R. to metal gate at top by fence/hedge,over stile here. Diag. L. to trees at top. On, keeping

From page 21

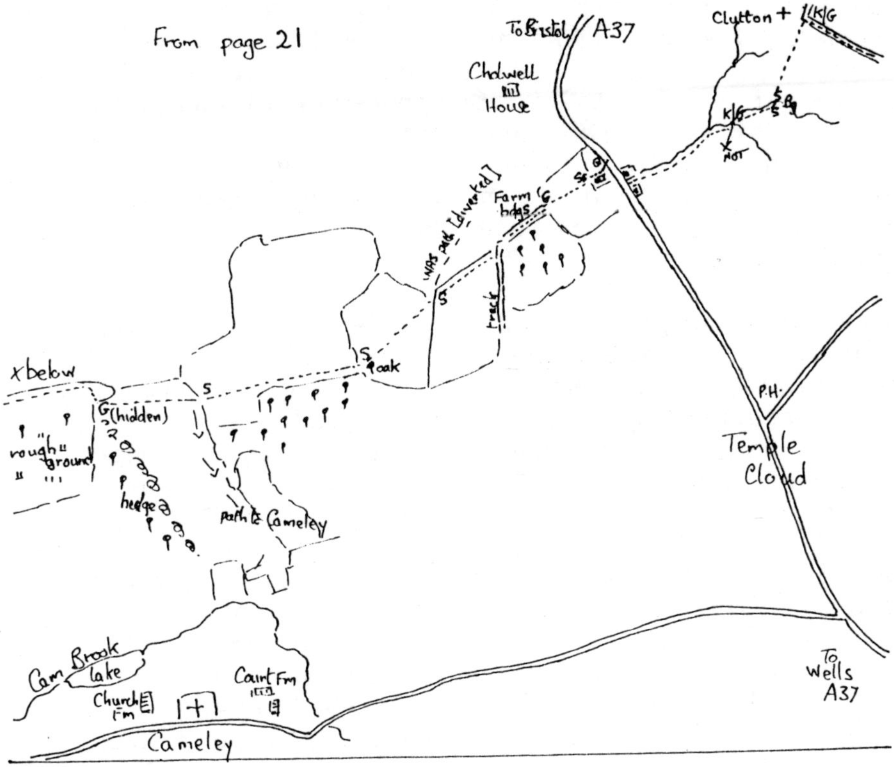

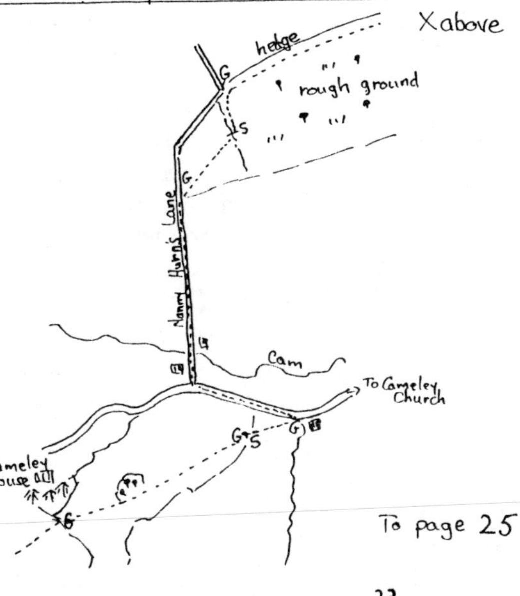

To page 25

trees on your R., and slightly R. to gate in far corner of field. Cross next 2 fields & 2 stiles. In third field go to R. corner of hedge ahead, where over stone stile. One more field and gate to road. T.R. up road and bear R. at fork. This is Hinton Blewett. Cross road at top to letter box and L. in front of pub. You now leave the Cam Brook which you have followed all the way from Midford.

Round two bends, church on R. Walk on road keeping R. at next two road junctions. On next bend (Prospect Stile, views here), over stile in front; do not start walking downhill on road. Down very steeply diag. L. to post. Here stile in hedge below is visible. Scramble down to this and cross, forward to next stile ahead (hedge on your R.).

You may hear the hydraulic ram operating - follow buried water pipe down hill and out onto road at gate (O.S. map differs here). * T.R. and immed. L. by wooden field gate into garden of Heyden's Farm. Walk down by side of house to stile in fence ahead into field. Where L.H. hedge starts to bend R. go through stile in it and continue along other side of hedge via iron gate, then a stone stile by stream, to road.

T.R. along road, past houses, and one field further on through iron gate on R. Round large field keeping fairly near R.H. hedge towards building seen across field. The stile is in the far hedge opposite the near end of the building enclosure (one hedge removed here). Then stone bridge over stream and forward to lane. It is not necessary to use stile and path to L. of, and beside, lane. Down this lane for ½ mile to West Harptree Square.

From page 23

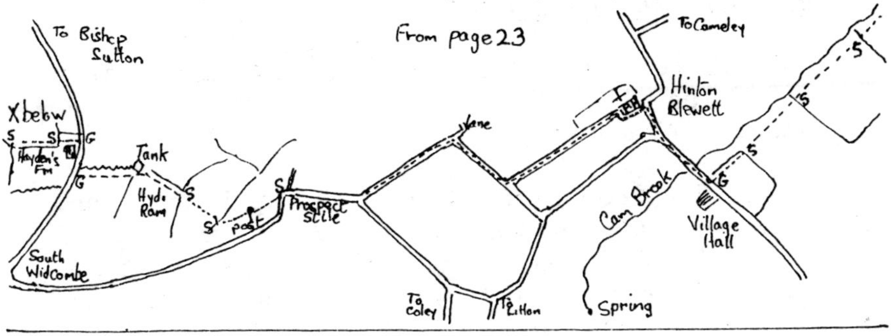

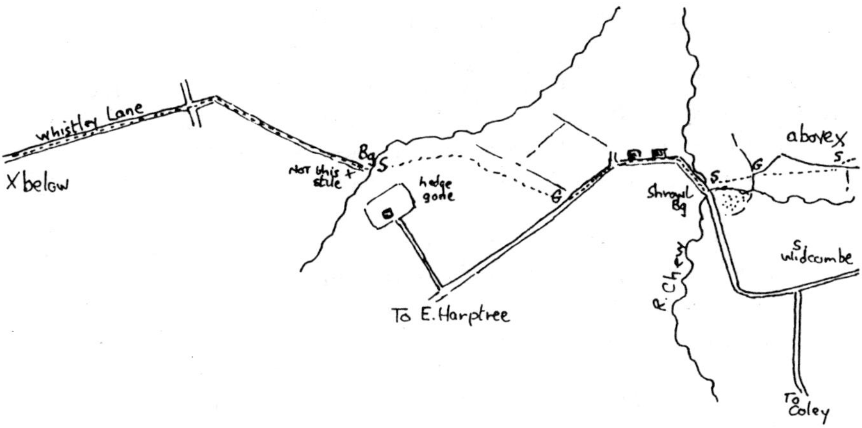

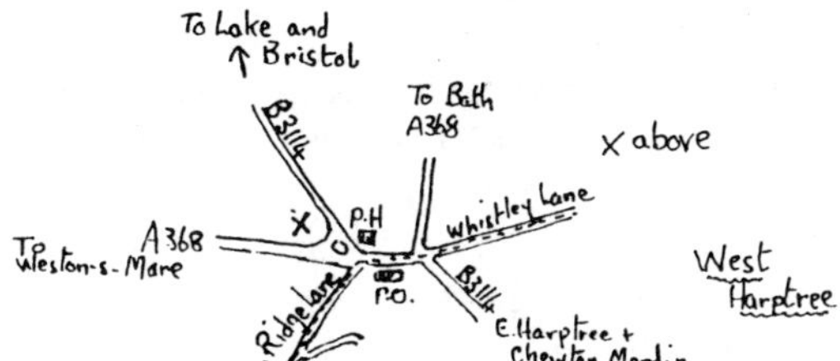

To page 27

6. West Harptree to Shipham

A climb up to the top of Mendip, with good views over to Wales if clear.
Distance: 10 miles

From West Harptree post office T.L. up Ridge Lane. Opp. last houses on your L. go over stile on R. by gate. Diag. L. to corner of wall, over stile, diag. R. towards buildings. In the dip, over double stile and stone bridge and up ahead over 2 more stiles into sunken lane. **

Diag. R. over field to iron gate at L. of bungalow. Take the R.H. of the 2 lanes (Cowleaze Lane) which in about ¼ mile comes out on Harptree Hill. This lane may be impassable in summer -if so, from **

> Sharp L. keeping by hedge. At end of hedge straight over field through gate in fence (not on O.S.map) then diag.L. over next field, out by gate to lane. T.R. up lane, 1st turn R., R. again and finally R. down Harptree Hill. Round the bend join main route.

To continue with official route: emerging from Cowleaze Lane, L. up hill and immed. R. by broken iron gate on track into field. Bear R. to hedge opp. by pole, on with hedge on your R. Near end of field, over stile on R. and steeply down over narrow rough field to stile onto lane, where T.R.

Just past houses on L., lane bends R. ON the bend through wooden gate on L. into bottom of a garden. On with wall on your R., through small wood, out by bungalows, down driveway onto lane. (If walking the other way, go up driveway on your R. by tall cupressus, then small path on L. past first bungalow).

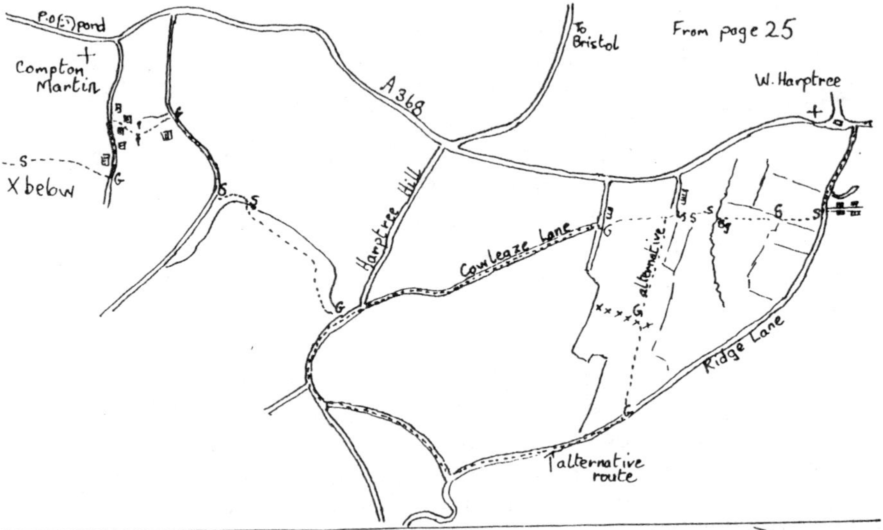
P.O. pond
Compton Martin
X below
To Bristol
A368
From page 25
W. Harptree
Harptree Hill
Cowleaze Lane
alternative
Ridge Lane
alternative route

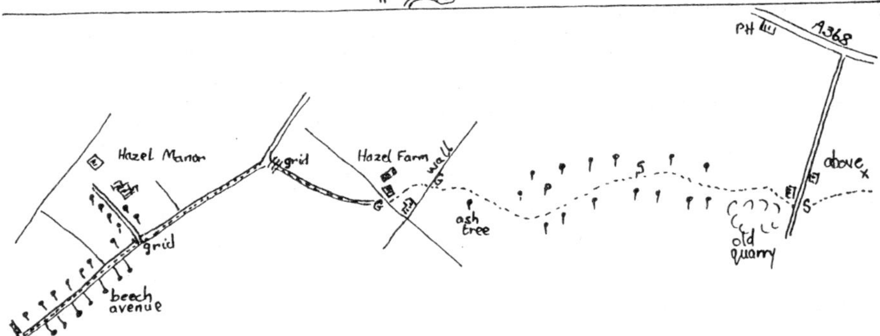
PH
A368
Hazel Manor
grid
Hazel Farm
wall
ash tree
old quarry
above x
grid
beech avenue

To page 29

To visit Compton Martin (church, P.O. stores and pub) T.R. Otherwise, T.L. up lane and past last house on R. before cattle grid, take R.H. gate and walk behind house with fence, later hedge, on your R. Keep up on a slight ridge to stile at end in R.H. corner. Then stile to lane and up small path opp. to L. of garden gate. If you have been to the village, rejoin route here by coming up this lane, which starts just east of the pub.

Pass old quarry and climb up through woods, stile part way up. Emerge from wood into field and climb by ash tree to stone wall which soon becomes visible (Hazel Farm). Through small gate in wall on your R., cross farmyard diag.L. between house and barns, through gate and R. down driveway. Over cattle grid and T.L. Pass Hazel Manor drive, over cattle grid and just after a house in front comes into view, T.R. down Green Lane.

After about ½ mile lane turns sharp R. at stile and gate, then sharp L. (see round barrows in field on R.), past Ubley Hill Farmhouse to T-junction with Ubley Drove. By iron gate opp. into field and on by R.H. hedge. Stile into Leaze Lane which in about ½ mile bends R. At Leaze Farm T.L. on tarmac drive to road (called 'Two Trees').

T.R. down the hill. At junction, ½ mile down the hill is Blagdon which has pubs and shops. The path, however, goes up the small lane opp. (NOT the road L.). At the end of wood on your R. go through iron gate. Now follow hedge on your L. via 3 fields and gates and emerge onto rough ground. Here, sharp L. and down path through bushes to car park at top of Burrington Combe. (There is often an ice-cream van here).

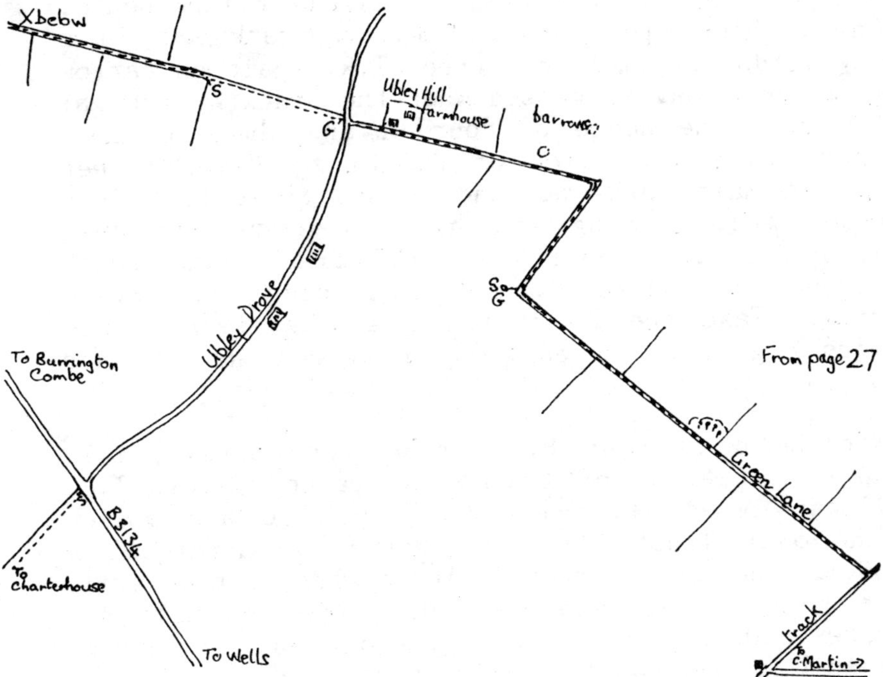
X below
S
G
Ubley Hill
farmhouse
barrows
So
G
Ubley Drove
To Burrington
Combe
From page 27
Green Lane
To
Charterhouse
B3134
To Wells
track
To
C.Martin →

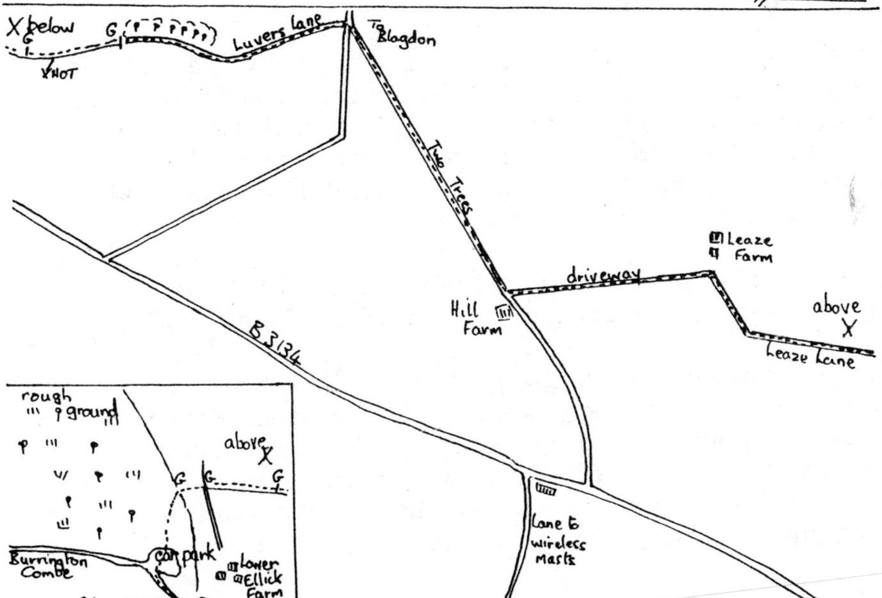
X below
G
X NOT
Luvers Lane
To
Blagdon
Two Trees
Leaze
Farm
driveway
Hill
Farm
above
X
Leaze Lane
B3134
rough
ground
above
X
G
car park
Burrington
Combe
Lower
Ellick
Farm
To page 31
Ellick
House
B3134
Lane to
wireless
masts

T.L. up road and R. on first track by Ellick House. On reaching open ground T.R. on track and in a few yards, by small oak tree, T.R. again on narrow path which may be missed when the bracken is high. Now keep the hedge on your R. and where it ends there is a good view of Burrington Combe. Keep on the main path, descend to and cross East Twin Brook and, keeping straight on, eventually West Twin Brook. Ignore all side tracks and reach T-junction. Here R. and soon cross very wide ride. Take the L. of the 2 tracks ahead, cross marshy ground and on to join main track at edge of wood.

With wood on your R. keep on for approx.$\frac{1}{4}$ mile until a meeting of tracks is reached, where T.R. Almost immed. L. over stile by gate and notice 'National Trust, Dolebury Warren'. Straight on until you reach corner of fence where ignore stile on your R. On ahead beside fence to stile and gate. At top of slope, turn off on R.H. track, then L. round <u>top</u> of conifer wood.

Cross open top of hill, via stile by gate, and keep on along crest of hill until you reach the east gate of the hillfort. Walk round stony mound in front of you and descend over rough ground, aiming for the green path in the distance. When you reach it, T.R. on it.

(Coming the other way, leave green path and climb up L. over rough ground to top of hillfort).

Go out through west gate of fort and bear L. down stony track through wood. Leave the Warren by a gate, down to track where T.L. by houses. At junction with lane, T.L. up lane, over stile by gate and straight on. Soon pass path on R. which goes up to join Rowberrow Lane near church.

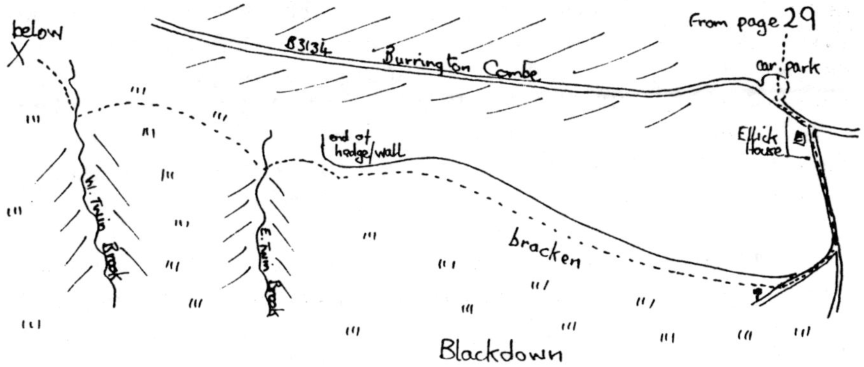
below
B3134
Burrington Combe
From page 29
car park
Ellick House
end of hedge/wall
W. Twin Brook
E. Twin Brook
bracken
Blackdown

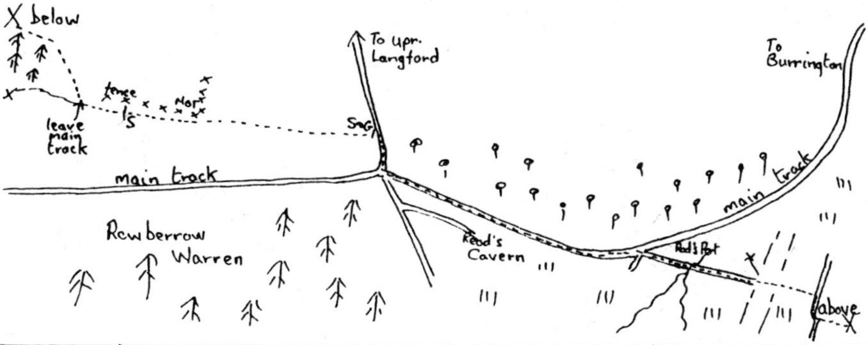
below
To Upr. Langford
To Burrington
fence
leave main track
main track
Rowberrow Warren
Read's Cavern
main track
above

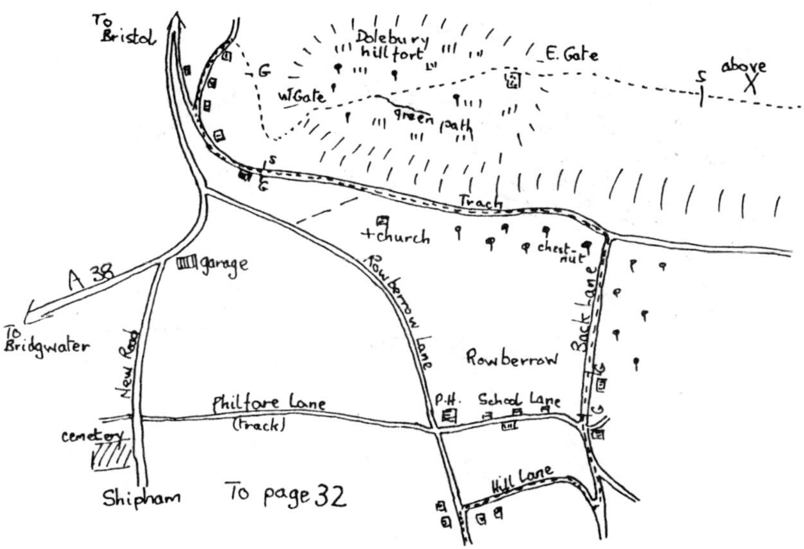
To Bristol
Dolebury hillfort
E. Gate
above
W. Gate
green path
Track
church
chest-nut
garage
A 38
To Bridgwater
Rowberrow Lane
Back Lane
Rowberrow
New Road
Philfore Lane
(Track)
P.H.
School Lane
cemetery
Hill Lane
Shipham
To page 32

Keep on <u>main</u> track and where it starts to rise T.R. up path by horse chestnut tree. This is Back Lane. Up lane, through metal gate at top. Ignore path up R. and keep on track past pink house and through another metal gate by a second house where a lane comes in from the R. Straight on here and soon T.R. up tarmac track.

A few yards further on, by large sycamore tree roots in R.H. bank, turn <u>sharp</u> R and double back up steep narrow path. Keep on until you reach Rowberrow Lane, where T.L. Continue on lane, which becomes Hollow Road and takes you to the centre of Shipham by the 'Miners Arms'.

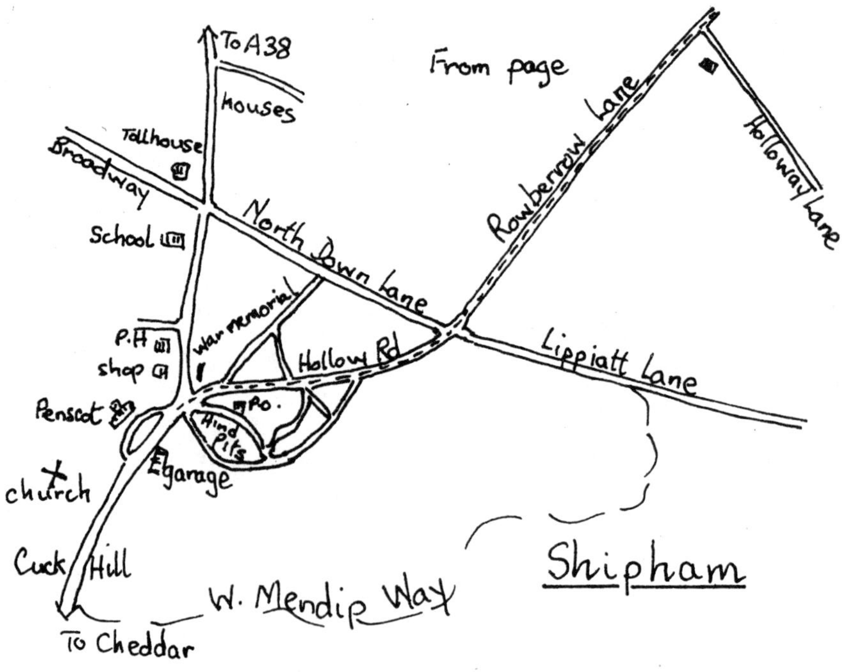

CIRCULAR WALKS

The following 12 walks are circular, using parts of the 'Link'. Wherever possible there are cafés or pubs on the routes so that walkers may have a pleasant day out. Day walkers will probably have more time to see the various places of interest en route than those walking the 'Link' from end to end.

For the circular walks it is useful to have the appropriate O.S. Pathfinder Series sheet, scale 1:25,000 ($2\frac{1}{2}$" to a mile), as well as the 'Limestone Link'. These maps may sometimes be borrowed from the library but if you intend to do more than one walk they are well worth buying.

1. On the Cotswold Way. A long walk from Bath. Get a bus to Weston (Bath) and walk the Cotswold Way to Cold Ashton, approx. $7\frac{1}{2}$ miles. Lunch stop at White Hart. Return via 'Link' to Batheaston, 5 miles, and bus back to Bath, or walk by R. Avon.

Canal Bridge, Bathampton

2. A Cream Tea Walk (café open Apl.to end Oct.) Walk 'Link' from beginning to 'stile by iron gate to road' at * (ST 783693). R. to road junction where T.R. passing tea gardens (on your R.) and continue on road past St. Catherine's Court. Keep L. at junction, up hill to Fry's Farm on your R. Up track between buildings here and keep on until you reach lane, T.R. back to Cold Ashton. 7 miles.

Maps needed for 1 and 2: ST 67/77 Bristol East
ST 66/76 Bath/Keynsham

3. Along the Canal. (a) Walk from the 'George' at Bathampton as far as the pumping station. Cross canal to Claverton and up to the American Museum. Then carry on up road and either take a bus from near the University or walk about 1 mile down Bathwick Hill. Return to canal towpath at bottom and walk east, returning to Bathampton.
(b) Walk from Bathampton to Dundas Basin on tow-path, lunch at Viaduct Hotel and return the same way. Pleasant in summer. Both about 7 miles.

4. The Old Canal and Locks. Start at Tucking Mill at * and follow 'Link' via Midford to Combe Hay (Wheatsheaf). Return via quiet lanes almost parallel with 'Link' path. 5 miles.

For Walks 3 and 4 map ST 66/76 Bath & Keynsham.

5. The Old Colliery Villages. Start at Dunkerton Bridge on A367 (easily reached by bus from Bath) and go down steps. Follow 'Link' to Camerton post office. Here T.L. to cross roads and take road to your L. Follow it through Wick Lane and up the hill to Carlingcott (pub). Then down again, crossing over 'Link' at bottom, and along lane back to Dunkerton Bridge. OR: from Camerton cross-roads go on up the hill and visit Skinner's church.

You can either continue up to A367 and get a bus back to Bath, or return to Camerton crossroads, or take a footpath from church over fields to Wick Lane. 5½ miles, or 4 if bus from Camerton.

6. Explore the Paulton Basin. Start at Radford and walk on 'Link' nearly to sewage works, but instead of going over F/B and round tip,take F/P north at Paulton Basin, over old railway track. Climb the hill to Timsbury (pub) and back to start via Mill Lane or Radford Hill. About 3 miles.

7. A Short Stroll. From Hallatrow follow 'Link' to the road at Bendal's Bridge just before Clutton church. T.L. along Marsh Lane & back to Hallatrow. You may care to explore Clutton before returning. 3 miles.
For walks 5,6, & 7: ST 65/75 Radstock & Wellow.

Gate to St James' Church, Cameley

8. Cameley's Redundant Church. Start where 'Link' crosses A37 soon after leaving Clutton (bus from Bristol). Follow it as far as (a) 'Ring of Bells' at Hinton Blewett. From here take the road north (towards Bishop Sutton) and immed. R. (signed 'Cameley'). This passes Cameley church. Continue on lane until A37 is reached, or take path on your L. which cuts off corner and comes out by Temple Cloud school. Either get bus back from here to Bristol or walk back to start on pavement. (b) The walk may be cut short by turning L. to Cameley church when you reach the road at the bottom of Nanny Hurn's Lane. 5 or 3 miles.

Maps: ST 65/75 Radstock/Wellow, ST 45/55 Cheddar.

9. Burledge Hillfort. Follow the 'Link' from Hinton Blewett to the lane past the hydraulic ram at*. T.R. along lane, soon unfenced - this is Widcombe Common. On reaching main A368 sharp R. up another lane and climb to hillfort. Views over Chew Valley Lake. (Birdwatchers should go L. on A368 a few hundred yards to Herriotts Bridge before returning to climb hillfort). Over fort, keep on down path to crossroads, T.R. to return to start. 4 miles.

10. On Top of Mendip. From 'Ring of Bells' at Compton Martin go up lane and join 'Link' as explained in walking instructions. On reaching Ubley Drove T.L. on it instead of going straight on, cross B3134 and stile opposite. This takes you to the Charterhouse lead mining site. Having looked round, take the green lane (on your L. as you came into the site, now on R.) back to B3134. Cross, up road opp. by house. Where road bends sharp R. (i.e. the 2nd bend) keep straight on up track back to Hazel Farm and start of walk. 6 miles.

To extend this walk, follow 'Link' to the road called 'Two Trees'. T.L. to B3134 where T.R. In a few yards by a house take track on your L. and climb to wireless masts. T.L. on track down to road where R. and immed. L. on F/P to mining site, then as above. 7 miles.

Stone Gate Posts, Hazel Manor

11. Burrington Combe and Dolebury. From car park at top of Combe follow 'Link' over Dolebury until route turns R. up Back Lane. Keep straight on instead, coming out of the valley at the meeting of paths. Take L.H. track ahead (i.e. do not turn L.) keeping along edge of wood. Track bends L., descends steeply, becomes tarmac lane and arrives down at Garden Centre (& café next door).

Cross road and up lane opposite. In $\frac{1}{3}$ mile take track steeply up R. at edge of wood, climb and cross open, rough ground, back to car park.
7 miles.

12. Burrington Combe & Beacon Batch. From the car park at the top of the Combe walk the 'Link' to the Miners Arms, Shipham. Back up Hollow Road, T.R. up Lippiatt Lane and follow W. Mendip Way to Tyning's Farm. T.L. and climb hill. Past wall, diag. R. on (muddy) track as far as Beacon Batch triangulation point. At over 1,000 ft. this is the highest point on Mendip, with extensive views. Straight down (north) to Ellick House and car park. 8 miles.

For Walks 9, 10, 11 & 12: ST 45/55 Cheddar.

The Manor House and Church of St Leonard, Shipham

COLD ASHTON. The 'Link' starts on the oolitic limestone of the Cotswolds, seen in the attractive buildings of this village. It is thought to have been John Gunning, Mayor of Bristol, who built the beautiful manor house about 1629 in a style befitting an important Bristol merchant. It was to this village - probably to the Rectory - that Sir Bevil Granville was brought to die during the Civil War after the Battle of Lansdown. The King's men lost many of their finest cavalry attacking the Roundheads in this broken and precipitous terrain. The Rectory, now a private house, was built about 1509.

A charter exists recording a grant made by King Aethelstan in AD 931 to Bath Abbey of 5 hides (a measure of land) at Aesctune, and names various points on the parish boundary.

Cold Ashton: gate to the Manor House

ST. CATHERINE'S VALLEY. St. Catherine's Brook rises near Marshfield and flows down to the former mill site where it is joined by its tributary stream. The latter starts at the springs just below Cold Ashton. The brook is fast-flowing, dropping 500 ft. in the few miles of its course, and so many water mills were working along it in days gone by. Apart from the one above, there was a mill near where the 'Link' first comes out on to a lane. This was a paper mill on Monkswood Brook and had a group of cottages nearby which have now been demolished. The 'Monkswood Hoard' of Bronze Age date found near here consisted of many kinds of bracelets and sickles.

Monkswood Reservoir was opened in 1896 to supply Bath; Monkswood Brook joins St. Catherine's at the next mill, Beek's; then there was a mill by Ayford Farm and several other sites down to Batheaston which had a paper mill.

The Court and Church: the monks of the Benedictine monastery of Bath built a grange, or manor house, church and fishponds in this quiet and remote valley. The present house dates from 1490 with additions from the 17th century. The fishponds were in the small side valley just to the north; the tithe barn remains.

The present church was built by Prior Cantelow of Bath about 1490. One of the stained glass windows shows him kneeling below St. John, with a request that people should pray for his soul.

Later the Court belonged to a godson of Queen Elizabeth, Sir John Harington of Kelston. In 1591 he leased, and later sold, the estate to John Blanchard, a wool merchant of Marshfield. There is an elaborate memorial in the church to his son William, died 1631.

The Blanchards built the terraced gardens and planted the yew hedges, also built a porch on the north front and made other extensions. In the 24.11.1906 issue of 'Country Life' there is an article by Gertrude Jekyll on the gardens,with many pictures of how they looked then.

The house fell into decline but was bought by Col.Strutt M.P. of Essex in 1841 and his family owned it for over 100 years. They restored the house and church and built a new farmhouse. The extension to the south-east dates from the present century. St. Catherine's spring flows up in an aperture in the retaining wall of the terrace.

BATHEASTON originally grew up on the west side of the brook above marshy ground, and modern houses have been built on the east side. The monks of Bath held an estate here too. Coming down the street, see Eagle House which John Wood the Elder partly rebuilt in 1729; see also Middlesex House and Pine House, late 17th century buildings.

For panoramic views climb Little Solsbury Hill by taking the turning opposite the R.C. church and then first right. This hillfort was occupied for 2-300 years before the Romans came and was defended by a ditch and rampart. Traces of houses have been excavated and many weaving combs and spindle whorls found up there. The name means 'Salt Hill', the A46 road nearby having been a medieval saltway.

As with many of the churches along the 'Link',that at Batheaston although an old foundation, is mostly Victorian apart from its tower. Several inns were built on the London-Bath turnpike, the A4, including the 'Lamb & Flag' dated 1770. In the time of Beau Nash passengers had to endure a long and dangerous journey in an unsprung coach to reach Bath. How glad they must have been to rattle down the hill into Batheaston, their destination within sight. Batheaston House may be seen from the river path, an imposing mansion, dated 1712.

BATHAMPTON. In the church, rebuilt by Ralph Allen in 1754, is buried Captain Arthur Phillip RN, who in 1786 was appointed Governor of the new colony of New South Wales with orders to form a penal settlement at Botany Bay. Sailing in May 1787, his company arrived there the following January. He decided that Botany Bay was unsuitable and took his party ashore at Sydney Cove,establishing the first settlement in Australia. The Australia Chapel and Phillip Memorial may be seen in the church.

THE KENNET & AVON CANAL was built to link Bath with Newbury on the R. Kennet and so join Bristol to Reading on the R. Thames. It was 57 miles long, with a staircase of 29 locks at Devizes - now being restored- and cost £950,000 to build. John Rennie was appointed Engineer and the canal was completed in 1810. It was a broad canal, taking not narrow boats but vessels up to 80 ft. long and 21 ft. wide each carrying over 50 tons - heavy goods such as coal, stone and lime. From the beginning it was very successful, by 1839 carrying 342,000 tons of goods a year. There was a dramatic drop in receipts between 1841 and 1842, when the railway began to compete. It was bought out by the railway in 1852 and gradually declined.

The beautiful Bath stone Dundas Aqueduct which takes the canal over the R. Avon was named after Charles Dundas who was largely responsible for the canal's success, and designed by Rennie. The 64 ft. arch is dated 1800. Just before the aqueduct there is a basin with a crane by Acraman of Bristol and a landing stage.

At this basin the K & A was joined by the Somerset Coal Canal at a lock, and this junction can now be seen, as the beginning of the SCC has been restored. The SCC and Railway will be described as a whole later on.

Dundas Basin, Kennet and Avon Canal

Claverton Pumping Station was built between 1809 and 1813 to supply the Nine Mile Pound, that is, the canal between the top of the locks at Widcombe (Bath) and the next lock at Bradford-on-Avon. The design was by John Rennie and the station was built on a site where river and canal are close. There had been a mill here since Saxon times and a weir and leat still remained.

The pumping station is waterwheel-powered; each wheel, with 48 buckets, has an overall diameter of 17'7". One lockful of water per hour can be pumped into the canal. Restoration work started in 1969 and now it is open to the public on summer Sundays and is working on certain weekends.

CLAVERTON MANOR. A new manor house was built on the hill above the village in 1819-20 by Sir Jeffry Wyatville. It now houses the American Museum and may be reached by crossing the canal by the pumping station and walking through Claverton village. It is open on summer afternoons: if you wish you can walk in the gardens and have tea on the terrace without going into the museum itself.

MIDFORD. The new turnpike road with a better gradient replaced the old steep road from Bath and it crosses the valley here near the junction of the Midford, Cam and Wellow brooks. The 'Castle' on the hill to the north was built c.1775 for Henry Roebuck. The plan is said to represent the ace of clubs, in commemoration of a win at cards.

There were two railway bridges over the road at Midford. That of the Camerton & Limpley Stoke Railway has been demolished. The one remaining was the track of the Somerset & Dorset Railway which terminated at Green Park station, Bath. This extension from Evercreech to Bath was opened in July 1874. The 8-arched brick and stone viaduct carried the S & D over the Bath-Frome road and the coal canal. The station platform may be seen from the pub carpark. The line closed in the 1960s and now it is difficult to imagine the 'Pines Express' on its way to Bournemouth on summer weekends. With two engines, it climbed the Chilcompton incline and crossed the top of Mendip.

COMBE HAY. The manor house, church and lake form an attractive group in a beautiful setting above the Cam Brook. The house dates partly from 1730 and partly 1770.

The Fosse Way passes just to the north-west of Combe Hay village and crosses the Cam Brook at Dunkerton Bridge. The original line for about 1½ miles north of the latter is now a footpath.

Excavations took place at Combe Hay following the discovery in 1968 at the fuller's earth mine of a Roman stone coffin and a possible pottery kiln. Later, other stone coffins containing skeletons were found. With its wooded valleys and many springs this was a good area for settlement and people were certainly living here in the Bronze Age. Romans were here early but the (possible) villa was rebuilt during the later Roman period, to be abandoned after 400 AD.

CAMERTON. The Fosse Way passes through the south end of Camerton where people had already been living for thousands of years. Roman Camerton was a small town, first with timber buildings but after 200 AD built of stone, when the inhabitants were engaged in pewter working. The area is at the junction of the road from Camerton village with the main Bath road, which here follows the course of the Fosse Way. A large Saxon cemetery was found about 200 yards to the south-west; although some graves contained Saxon objects, its origin is believed to be earlier. People were living here amongst the ruined buildings after the Romans left.

Read the Revd. John Skinner's 'Journal of a Somerset Rector' 1803-34 for a fascinating account of Camerton's people at this time. Skinner, born 1772, trained as a lawyer but was ordained in 1799, coming to the living of Camerton the year afterwards. He was totally unsuited to minister here and appears to have been incapable of communicating with his parishioners. In June 1822 he writes 'I am heartily sick of the flock over which I am nominated'. Yet he was well-meaning and compassionate to the poor, spending much time visiting the dying, but too much time in disputes with the farmers over tithes. He complains about the lack of respect with which he is treated, and could not even establish friendly relations with the churchwardens or parish clerk. He found solace in archaeological research, often working with Sir Richard Colt-Hoare of Stourhead.

New pit, Camerton

The parsonage and church were adjacent to the old court, until the early 18th century the seat of the Carew family. It then belonged to James Stephens, the colliery owner, whose daughter married a Jarrett, and so by 1800 the Jarretts owned the court. In 1835 they built the present court on a new site further from the church.

Skinner married in 1805 and had 5 children, two of whom survived him. In 1810 his brother and two sisters died, his wife in 1812, all of consumption, as many villagers did. Skinner's chief hate was the Methodists, now established in all the coalfield villages, followed by the Ale Houses, especially the Red Post and Camerton Inn.

A happier note is struck in June 1822 when he hired a coal barge equipped with an awning, tables and chairs, and took a party of 15 ladies and gentlemen for a cold collation at Combe Hay. His horse pulled the barge there along the canal from Paulton Basin through Camerton and on the way back musicians played.

There were many accidents in the mines: for example in March 1822 - Bull's son has broken his neck in the pit; March 1830 - 5 colliers killed by the breaking of a rope at Paulton. There was also great poverty, disease (e.g. cholera), immorality, irreligion and drunkenness to contend with. A diary entry, July 14, 1822, ref. morning service: 'the singers, who have been in a state of constant intoxication since yesterday, being offended because I would not suffer them to chant the service.... put on their hats and left the Church'. It appears that they went straight up to the Red Post and vowed in future to join the Methodists!

John Skinner should have remained a lawyer. He was his own worst enemy but conditions in Camerton were wellnigh impossible, and one cannot help feeling sorry for him. 'Truly', he writes, 'it may be said Society is now out of joint; what with Methodists, Catholics, Colliers, Servants and Attornies, all domestic comfort is estranged'. Also being estranged from his two sons, he began to deteriorate mentally after the end of his edited journals in 1834. In October 1839, having no more purpose in life, he took a gun to the woods and shot himself.

<u>THE SOMERSET COAL CANAL & RAILWAY</u>. The two have to be considered together because after the canal was closed the railway company used parts of its bed for their tracks. The junction of the SCC with the Dundas Basin has already been mentioned, and a small distance has recently been restored as a marina for pleasure boats. From here to Paulton Basin the 'Link' follows the canal route.

Tucking Mill - Memorial to William Smith

The canal was planned to take coal from the Somerset coalfield to the K & A Canal at Dundas. Acts were obtained in 1794 and 1796 and the first Engineer was William Smith 'the father of English geology', commemorated by a plaque on the Tucking Mill cottage which the 'Link' passes. (Tucking = fulling, and at one time there was a fuller's earth works here). A picture of 1890 shows the cottage on the canal side. Smith was dismissed in 1799.

The canal went as far as Paulton, but a second branch from Midford to Radstock was planned. However the locks up from Midford were never built and a horse tramway was used instead. The canal basin at Midford was the junction of the tramway and canal, and it had wharves, a weigh-house and a long, low aqueduct to carry the canal over the Cam Brook into this basin (to join up with tramway)

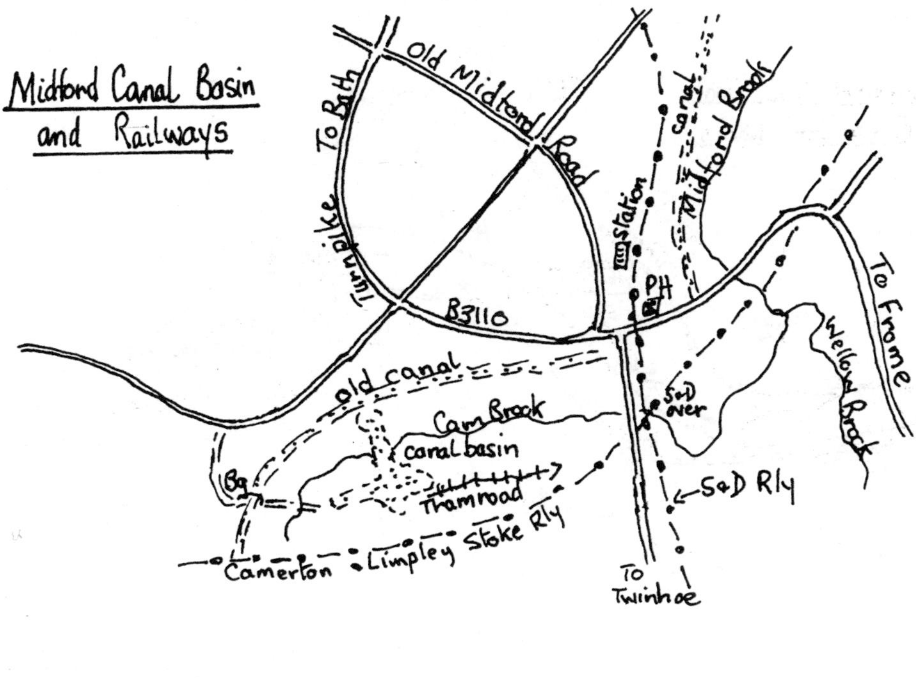

There was a considerable drop between the collieries and Dundas, so a boat lift, or caisson, was tried out to raise and lower boats. This was sited near Caisson House. The box (or caisson) was watertight and held the complete barge. In 1799 successful trials of this were watched by the Prince of Wales but later the idea had to be abandoned and an incline was constructed by Benjamin Outram. This involved transferring the coal twice and so a flight of 22 narrow locks was built at Combe Hay instead, opening in April 1805. To the west of Combe Hay there was a tunnel nearly 200 ft. long.

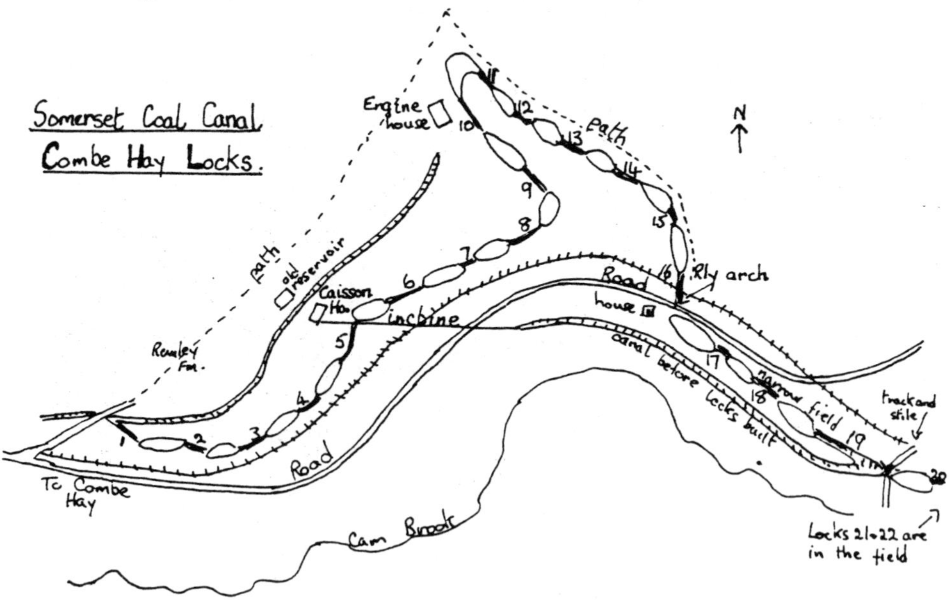

The inclined plane may be seen if walkers proceed on the road towards Combe Hay a short distance; the engine was probably sited in Engine Wood; and the locks can be found along the 'Link'. The footpath shown on the O.S. map to the east of that used by the 'Link', coming down from Engine Wood, was the line of the feeder canal. Caisson House was built in the late 18th century for John Smith, alias Leigh, and lived in from 1813 by the William Hills, father and son, engineers to the company. The father died in 1868 at the age of 92 and was buried in Combe Hay churchyard. His son retired in 1882, aged 70.

By 1850, 23 pits were joined to the canal by tramroads. It was extremely prosperous until the 1870s when the Bristol & North Somerset line opened to Radstock. In 1883 the B & N.S. opened a 3½ mile long branch from their line at Hallatrow to serve the Camerton collieries, duplicating the line of the canal. The Somerset & Dorset bought the tramway route of the Radstock arm of the canal for its own line. Another reason for the SCC's decline was that it depended solely on the collieries, and many of the original pits had closed. So the canal ceased to be used in 1898 and in 1904 the GWR bought it and built a railway, using the canal route wherever possible.

This railway, the 'Camerton & Limpley Stoke', ran from 1907 and joined the Hallatrow branch at Camerton. It crossed the Cam Brook at Midford and used the canal tunnel at Combe Hay, having stations at Dunkerton and Monkton Combe and halts at Radford, Timsbury and Combe Hay. Later, halts were opened at Paulton and Midford. This single line joined the GWR at Limpley Stoke. Although a few passenger trains ran, the railway was mainly a coal outlet. Fortunately, some new collieries were opening at this time. In the year 1920,

$1\frac{3}{4}$ million tons of coal were mined at 26 pits and 7,387 people employed. By 1947, 13 pits produced $\frac{1}{2}$ million tons, employing 3,000.

In 1952 the film 'The Titfield Thunderbolt' was filmed on this line, using Monkton Combe station.

Somerset Coal Canal, Lock No. 15

THE SOMERSET COALFIELD. There were about 80 pits, not of course all working at the same time. Those near the 'Link' are mentioned below, the remainder being mostly to the south. Mining was going on quite extensively in the 16th and 17th centuries, but by the 1790s deeper pits were being sunk. Transport was a problem until the SCC and Radstock tramroad opened. The peak years were 1900-1920 but mines were not modernised and the 12 left working were nationalised 1.1.1947. By 1959 only 5 pits remained, and the last one closed in the early 1970s.

1. Dunkerton pit was the largest in Somerset with the worst reputation for working conditions and disregard for safety. There were riots in 1908-9. Railway sidings built c.1906, by 1912 over 700 miners. Closed 1927.

2. Camerton. James Stephens (of the Court) had a lease for 2 pits in 1781. The Old Pit was sunk, followed by the New Pit by 1800. Pits owned until 1911 by Jarretts. A large explosion in 1893 killed 2 men. Old Pit closed 1898. Maximum output was in 1903, c.77,000 tons. It was not modernised before nationalisation in 1947 and its accessible reserves were exhausted, so closed 1950.

3. Lower Conygre, just N. of Radford - had wharf on canal and later siding to railway. Dates 1848 until flooded in 1914.

4. Radford New Coal Work in 1793, had tramroad to canal, closed by 1847.

5. Withy Mills open by 1815 and shut by 1877. About 1850, 9 men killed. The lessor of the land was William Rees-Mogg.

6. Goosard Pit, alias Gooseward or Goosewardsham Pit or Paulton Lower Engine. Possibly sunk in 1708. Site is now the sewage works by Paulton Basin.

7. Paulton Engine Colliery - beside Paulton Foundry - one of the earliest in the area. Closed 1869. Four men and a boy killed by a rope breaking in 1830.

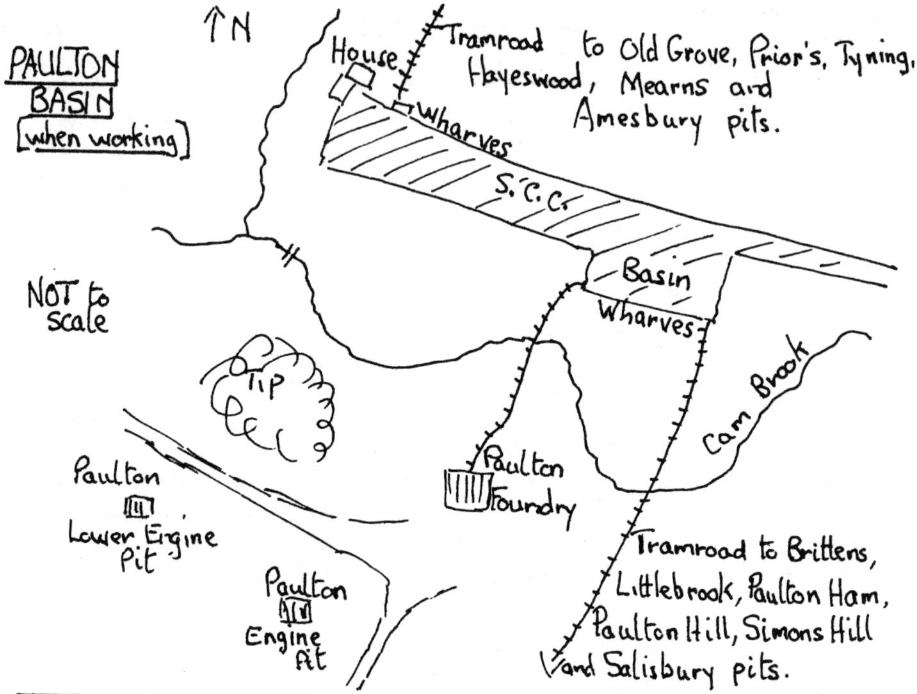

N
PAULTON BASIN
[when working]
House
Tramroad to Old Grove, Prior's, Tyning, Hayeswood, Mearns and Amesbury pits.
Wharves
S.C.C.
Basin
Wharves
NOT to scale
Tip
Cam Brook
Paulton Lower Engine Pit
Paulton Foundry
Paulton Engine Pit
Tramroad to Brittens, Littlebrook, Paulton Ham, Paulton Hill, Simons Hill and Salisbury pits.

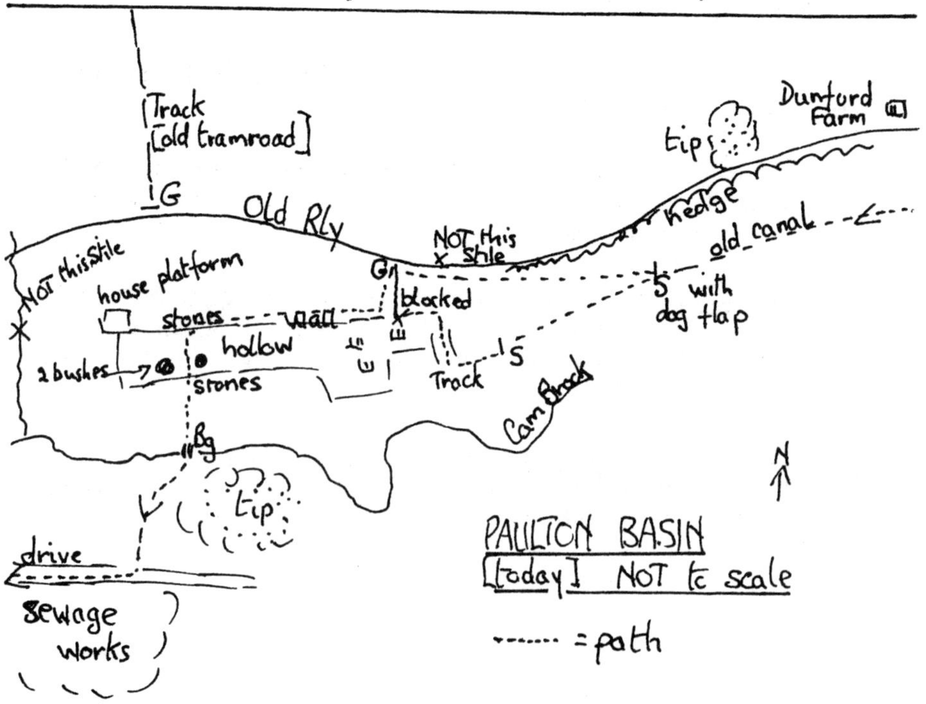

Track [old tramroad]
G
Old Rly
Dunford Farm
Tip
hedge
old canal
NOT this stile
NOT this stile
house platform
stones
wall
G
blocked
S with dog flap
hollow
2 bushes
stones
Track
S
Cam Brook
Bg
Tip
N
drive
PAULTON BASIN
[today] NOT to scale
= path
sewage works

8. Greyfield Pit - the track followed by the 'Link' from Hallatrow through the wooded gorge leads to this pit, the 'Link' turning off left before it is reached. The land for all the Clutton pits was leased by the Earl of Warwick and the Rees-Moggs were also shareholders. Closed 1911. A pit by Clutton station closed 1921 and one at Fry's Bottom to the north of Clutton in 1895.

Paulton Brass & Iron Foundry. Established 1810 and worked until 1890s building winding and pumping engines - one of their winding engines is in Bristol City Museum. Also made cast iron gateposts. Adjacent to, and south of, Paulton Basin.

Clutton - in spite of being a colliery village was an old settlement, the church having a 12th century doorway and chancel arch.

CAMELEY. In this tiny hamlet is a jewel among churches and it is certainly worth a small detour to see. The church is now redundant and usually unlocked. It has 2 galleries, built 1711 & 1819, a Norman font, 15th century benchends and a Jacobean pulpit with tester, reader's desk and family pew. There are also wall paintings.

Temple Cloud nearby grew in importance because it was on the turnpike road which bypassed Cameley, and it had a magistrates' court.

HINTON BLEWETT church also has a Norman font. 'Blewett' is a family name. Because of the regular village plan it is possible that it was laid out deliberately, and these planned settlements usually date from the 10th to 12th centuries. See also East Harptree. A couple of miles to the north is the hillfort of Burledge overlooking the Chew Valley Reservoir, opened by the Queen in 1956.

St Margaret's Church and the 'Ring O Bells', Hinton Blewett

At Prospect Stile the 'Link', having come over the watershed, descends into the Chew Valley past springs and hydraulic rams.

THE MANOR OF WIDCOMBE - not to be confused with the place of the same name in Bath - lies in four parishes but is mostly in West Harptree. Heyden's Farm, on the path but now re-named, was at the south end of the manor which stretches north to Herriotts Bridge on the lake. The farm was named after Thomas Heydon, tenant in 1611, although the house has since been completely rebuilt.

On a map of 1793 a footpath (now the 'Link')crosses the manor boundary at ST 57935684, and this is the site of Broad Close Stile mentioned in Norden's

Perambulation of 1611. Many of the farms and cottages standing at the time of the Perambulation have disappeared. The present Shrowl Bridge over the R. Chew was rebuilt this century a little upstream from the ancient one. The 'Link' crosses the very flat valley of the R. Chew, devoid of houses because it was liable to flooding.

WEST HARPTREE & COMPTON MARTIN are villages at the northern edge of Mendip. They stand on a line of springs, as the 'Link' has now reached the Carboniferous Limestone. The heavy rainfall on the hilltop sinks down through the limestone to emerge as springs at the bottom. Except for Blackdown - not limestone - there is almost no surface water on top. Until 1974 all these parishes were long and narrow, each having a piece on the flat, on the slope and on the top. The latter was unenclosed common land, used for sheep grazing and lead mining until about 200 years ago.

West Harptree (the name comes from the de Harpetre family) has two manor houses of the early and mid-17th century, Gournay Court and across the road, Tilley Manor House. East Harptree has the more interesting church, complete with monument to Sir John Newton, died 1568, with his wife and 20 children. Up the combe behind the village was Richmont Castle, destroyed during the wars of Stephen and Matilda. Nearby in 1887 a large Roman coin hoard was found in a pewter vessel.

Compton Martin takes its name from Robert Martin, the owner in the time of Henry I. The pond was used until 1840 by a paper mill, and here the R. Yeo rises, to flow via Blagdon Lake, Wrington and Congresbury to the Bristol Channel. Beside the pond the old farmhouse and out-buildings have recently been converted into houses.

The church is the thing to see here - usually open, but if not enquire at the post office. As you approach, look up and see the Norman corbel table with its strange carvings. Inside, the aisle arcades, chancel and font are Norman and there is a curious 'twisted' pillar. The 13th century effigy of Sir Thomas de Moreton has recently been restored. He held the Manor of Moreton, now under the Chew Valley Lake. There is another combe of limestone behind this village.

The Pond, Compton Martin

<u>THE TOP OF MENDIP</u>. Evidence of lead mining can be seen everywhere and there are also over 400 Bronze Age burial mounds. These were often used as parish boundary markers because they were about the only landmarks. One was used by the Roman surveyor aligning his road from the Charterhouse lead mines. This road ran south of the B3134.

The site of the Roman fortlet and amphitheatre can be seen at Charterhouse but the remains of lead mining there, including the horizontal chimneys, date from the 19th century re-smelting.

The land up on top was enclosed into large fields about 200 years ago and roads were built. Some of these, now lanes, are used by the 'Link' between Hazel Manor and Blagdon. Eventually people moved up from the villages onto their new lands and built their farms. All but a very few of the present-day farm buildings on the top of Mendip date from that time. Hazel Manor was burned down in 1929 when it was used as a shooting lodge. Previously it was owned by the Ennor family who came from Cornwall to rework the old lead slag. The farm still remains. See R.Atthill 'Old Mendip'.

Burrington Combe is a centre of caving. The caves were formed by rainwater sinking down and dissolving the limestone, and many are old subterranean river courses. Stone Age people lived in these caves and before them animals such as mammoth, hyena, bear and elephant. Some caves,Read's and Rowberrow, were inhabited during the Iron Age.

The 'Link' skirts round the edge of Blackdown,at over 1,000 ft. the highest point. As mentioned above, this is wet heather and peat moorland,not limestone. The path crosses the East and West Twin Brooks, which disappear down swallets on reaching the limestone, and passes near Goatchurch Cavern, Rod's Pot and Read's Cavern.

Dolebury Hillfort & Warren: this is a large Iron Age hillfort which has not been excavated. From the top may be seen other forts - Worlebury, Brean Down and Cadbury (Congresbury), also the Welsh coast. The remains of the warrener's house are just inside the fort's east gate, at the highest point. Warrens were deliberately made to encourage rabbits and 'pillow mounds' - long mounds of earth- were built for the rabbits to burrow and breed. There are 8 of these in the fort,5 are north-south and 3 east-west.

SHIPHAM & ROWBERROW. Rowberrow was noted for the production of calamine, last worked in 1853. It was carbonate of zinc and, mixed with copper, produced brass at the Bristol foundries. In 1790 it was said that fumes from the smelting had killed most of the trees. There were many more cottages in the valley and up by the old school than there are now. Rowberrow Warren was open land before it was planted with conifers.

Shipham (sheep farm) was a wild and lawless place in the mining days. Hannah More did much for the poor here and set up a Sunday School in the 1790s. She described the people as 'savage and depraved, brutal in their natures and ferocious in their manners'. She is commemorated by a window in the church (rebuilt in 1842).

Old Shipham consists of a network of lanes and cottages because mining shafts were sunk haphazardly with entrances sometimes in the backyards of cottages. Notice the road name 'Hind Pits'. Singing River Mine was a calamine working, the shaft entrances being on the opposite side of the road from the church and a short way up the hill, in a field. The mine was large and consisted of a vast network of underground galleries.

The route from Shipham via Lippiatt Lane and Holloway Rocks, now part of the West Mendip Way, was used by men walking to work at the Charterhouse lead-smelting site, and was known as the 'Slaggers Path'.

USEFUL INFORMATION

Bath Tourist Information Centre,
Guildhall, High Street, Bath.
(0225) 462831.

Wansdyke Council, Tourism Officer,
The Hollies, Midsomer Norton BA3 2DP.
(0761) 417510
Wansdyke Council Official Guide.

Kennet & Avon Canal Trust,
Couch Lane, Devizes, Wilts.
(0380) 71279
Twelve towpath guides and other literature about the canal available.

Cotswold Way Information:
Cotswold AONB Warden Service,
c/o County Planning Dept., Shire Hall,
Gloucester GL1 2TN. (0452) 425000

'The Cotswold Way - a Walker's Guide' by Mark Richards (Penguin) for details of route.

West Mendip Way:
Guidebook of this name available from Weston-s-Mare Civic Society, Heritage Centre, Wadham Street, Weston-s-Mare BS23 1JY. (0934) 412144

An extension from Wells to Shepton Mallet is sign-posted - write to Tourist Office at Wells, Somerset, for details. A further extension is planned from Shepton Mallet - Frome - Warminster to join the Ridgeway. Details eventually from Tourist Information Office, Frome, Somerset.

Avon Walkway (Bathampton to mouth of R.Avon): map from Avon.C.C. Planning Dept., Bristol.

TRANSPORT

British Rail

Bristol Temple Meads	(0272) 294255
Bath Station	(0225) 463075
Weston-s-Mare Station	(0934) 621131

Bus Services

Cold Ashton	Andrews Coaches of Marshfield (0225) 891212.Infrequent service from Bristol(outside John Lewis) to Marshfield. Alight on A420 at White Hart.
Shipham	Axe Vale Coaches, Edingworth. (0934)750321. Service 490 Bristol to Burnham-on-Sea. Badgerline Service 820/1 Bristol to Weston,two a day early and late to Shipham, but 2-hourly to Churchill Gate ($1\frac{1}{2}$ mls.away)
Batheaston	From Bath, Services 3,13,23,33 every 10 minutes.
Claverton Down (University) from B.R.Stn.	Badgerline Service 18, every 5 mins daytime, 15 mins w/ends.
Bathampton Claverton & Viaduct Hotel from Bath.	Badgerline Service 755/6, one a day, not Sunday. Services 264/5 Trowbridge/Frome. Frequent & Sunday service.
Dunkerton Camerton Turn Combe Hay Turn	Badgerline Service 173 Bath/ Wells, hourly. Services 176/184 Bath-Shepton Mallet or Frome, 2-hourly.

Clutton Temple Cloud	Badgerline Services 666/766 Bristol-Radstock-Bath, not Sunday Infrequent. Badgerline Service 376 Bristol-S.Mallet/Wells, hourly. On Sun. run by Southern National Service 676/7 2-hourly. Afternoons only.
Hallatrow Paulton (also Dunkerton)	Badgerline Services 177/179 Bath-Paulton-Bath. Service 178 Bath/Paulton/Bristol hourly, not Sunday.
W. Harptree C. Martin Burrington Turn	Badgerline Services 673/4/5 from Bristol. Not Sun., only 2-3 a day, not between 10 a.m. and 4 p.m.

Badgerline Ltd., Oldmixon Crescent,
Weston-s-Mare BS24 9AX (0934) 416171

Enquiries: Bath (0225) 464446
Bristol (0272) 297979
Weston-s-Mare (0934) 621201

Most buses from Bath and Bristol start from the bus stations. In Bath this is next to the B.R. station, but in Bristol about 1 mile away. Some but not all buses pass it.

Do not rely on the above information without first checking it.

FOOD, DRINK & ACCOMMODATION

Cold Ashton
White Hart, on main road, no accom. (0225) 891233

Batheaston
Mead Tea Gardens,St.Catherine's Valley, open Easter to end Oct. Also B/B. (0225) 858497

The North End - B/B & food, path passes door.

George & Dragon (0225) 858365

White Lion (0225) 858018. Both on path.

Bathampton
George Inn - food & garden on canal bank (0225) 425079

Monkton Combe
The Viaduct Hotel - by traffic lights after Dundas Basin. B/B & food. (0225) 723187

Midford
Hope & Anchor - restaurant. (0225) 832296

Mrs. Cross, Clearbrook Farm, Midford BA2 7DE.
B/B, no dinner. 022-122-3227
Shown on O.S. map as Midford Hill Farm.

Hallatrow
The Old Station - food & B/B. (0761) 52228

Temple Cloud
The Temple Inn - food & B/B. (0761) 52244

Clutton
The Warwick Arms (0761) 52256
The Railway Inn (0761) 52444

Hinton Blewett
Ring of Bells - food. (0761) 52239

West Harptree
Crown Inn. (0761) 221432

East Harptree
Waldegrave Arms - food. (0761) 221429

Mrs. Dearsley, Prospect House. B/B (0761) 221571
About ¾ mile off route.

Compton Martin
Ring of Bells - food. (0761) 221284

Blagdon
Seymour Arms (0761) 62279
Queen Adelaide (0761) 62573
Both serve food.

Rowberrow
The Swan Inn

Shipham
Miners Arms - food. (093-484) 2146

The Penscot Farmhouse Hotel - accom. (093-484) 2659.

One or two pubs passed have been omitted because they do not welcome walkers.

SHOPS

There are shops at Batheaston, post office stores at Camerton, Hallatrow, West Harptree and Compton Martin. Shops and post office at Blagdon and Shipham.

BOOKS TO READ

The City of Bath - Barry Cunliffe 1986

Archaeology of Avon - M.Aston & R.Iles (Avon C.C.)

Journals of Bristol Industrial Archaeology Society

Journals of Bristol & Avon Arch. Research Group, including Parish Survey of Cold Ashton.

Journals of Somerset Archaeological & N.H. Society

Little Solsbury, Avon: a National Trust pamphlet

Famous Houses of the West Country - C. Greenwood

Kennet & Avon Canal - K.R. Clew (David & Charles)

Somerset Coal Canal & Railways - K.R. Clew 1970 (David & Charles)

History of the Somerset Coalfield - Down & Warrington (David & Charles)

Somerset & Dorset Rly. - R.Atthill (David/Charles)

Journal of a Somerset Rector 1803-1834 ed. Coombs (Kingsmead 1971). Skinner's diary.

The Manor of Widcombe - ed.V.Russett (Avon C.C.)

Old Mendip - R.Atthill (David/Charles 2nd edn.1971)

Mendip, a New Study - ed.R.Atthill (David/Chs.1976)

Heart of Mendip - F.A.Knight,1st publ.1915, reprint 1971. Interesting pictures and descriptions.

Many of these books will be out of print and will have to be ordered from your library.